TAKE
CARE
OF
YOUR
FRIENDS

TAKE
an Enneagram guide

CARE

OF

YOUR
to interpersonal relationships

FRIENDS

CHRISTINA WILCOX

Andrews McMeel
PUBLISHING®

Andrews McMeel Publishing
a division of Andrews McMeel Universal
1130 Walnut Street, Kansas City, Missouri 64106

www.andrewsmcmeel.com

24 25 26 27 28 TEN 10 9 8 7 6 5 4 3 2 1

ISBN: 978-1-5248-8670-7

Library of Congress Control Number: 2024930408

Editor: Katie Gould
Designer: Holly Swayne
Production Editor: Jennifer Straub
Production Manager: Tamara Haus

CONTENTS

INTRODUCTION

I tend to minimize the writing I do regarding the Enneagram. My first book, *Take Care of Your Type*, wasn't some hard-hitting memoir about my trauma or a journey through the Alaskan tundra. It was practical and approachable, something to pick up on a lazy Sunday afternoon to later use to decorate your coffee table. I obviously put hard work into that book, but I wasn't finding myself bleeding for it. However, I've found myself bleeding for this book you're holding. It happened suddenly, looking down and realizing the stains I was leaving behind.

When I chose the concept of *Take Care of Your Friends,* my husband, Noah, and I had a conversation about how I wanted to do research for the project. I wanted to dive deep into the psychology of community to fuel my writing; I wanted to have a hard-hitting, memoir-esque book about the Enneagram and friendship. Noah pointed out, amid my excitement, how important it was going to be for me to focus on my friendships throughout writing this book. "I'll just have to take really good care of my friends," I thought. "Better than I ever have." I thought of the gatherings I would host and the stories of others I would get to know. Understanding others is what drew me to the Enneagram in the first place!

My drive to examine *how* to take care of my friends led to me desperately needing care *from* my friends. I became the friend in the pit, struggling with grief and mental health, embarrassed and confused.

My drive to examine how to take care of my friends led to me ironically, desperately needing care from my friends. I became the friend in the pit, struggling with grief and confusion around my purpose. And though the Enneagram did not magically heal my emotions or patch up my situations to perfection, it gave both myself and my friends a map to face uncharted territory.

So yes, I bled for this book. I should've known that seeking out to write a book about friendship would change me and my relationships; thankfully for the better! I am warning you that there may be something in here that you need to read but don't want to accept yet. You may find hidden clues as to why certain friendships failed or why some of them blossomed. If you find yourself bleeding from what the Enneagram can reveal as I did, I hope it is because this book found you exactly at the right time. The Enneagram is not a life-saving gospel, but it can be a compass; directing us to more compassion and grace for each other. Let's learn to take care of each other better, together!

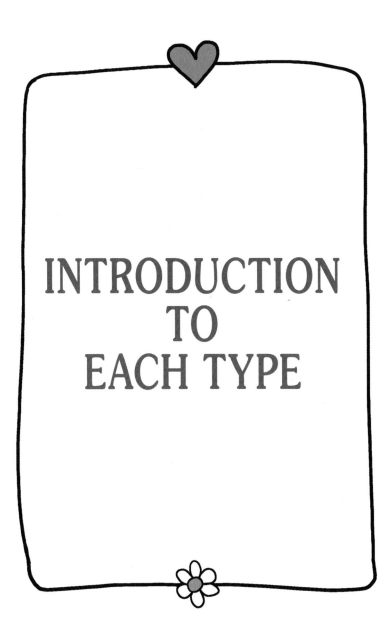

INTRODUCTION
TO
EACH TYPE

Enneagram Basics

With the wide variety of personality tests available online, I believe the Enneagram is unique because of its ability to make others feel understood. We all know that people are complex human beings who cannot fit into a personality typing system, but the Enneagram gets close to encompassing a lot of what makes humans human. Underneath our individual, specific needs are broader desires that we can each empathize with. Desires of . . .

- Goodness
- Love
- Admiration
- Significance
- Usefulness
- Safety
- Satisfaction
- Control
- Peace

It is within these desires that we find parts of ourselves. Maybe they're parts that we've neglected for a long time. Resurrecting the parts of ourselves we feel out of touch with allows us to show up fully in our relationships. Because, as opposed to only half of us being present, we now have our whole selves available and aware. By better understanding ourselves, we can better understand the type of friend we are and want to be.

Enneagram 1: The Improver

Core desire: To be good, to be beyond condemnation, to maintain balance and integrity

Core fear: Being condemned, corrupted, or evil

Enneagram 1s are not just perfectionists—they are people who crave adventure as well as goodness. They want to have adventure in their lives, but they feel as though they can't until goodness is achieved, or they are perfect enough for the things that life is offering them. This can be a slippery slope, because their rigidity can begin to sabotage not only themselves but also those they love. Because of the high standard they have for themselves, they can become resentful at the joy they see in others when others embrace life imperfectly. Understandably, this can be frustrating when they place their entire worth and value on how good, morally, they measure in comparison to those they love and look up to.

Enneagram 2: The Giver

Core desire: To be desired, worthy of love, and irreplaceable in the lives of
others
Core fear: Being replaceable, an obligation, and unworthy of love

Enneagram 2s are not just helpers—they are people who crave their own
empowerment separate from how they relate to others. Until they believe they
cannot be replaced, Enneagram 2s might exchange real, raw relationships for
imbalanced ones that rely more on their ability to give and sacrifice than resemble two humans in friendship with each other. This can be a slippery slope,
and it means 2s can lose out on all that true friendship has to offer them, like
giving to others while expecting nothing in return. However, Givers can also be
engaging, fierce leaders, filling their relationships with compassion and creativity. While they continually learn that there is no "right way" to love, they never
fail to love hard and warmly.

Enneagram 3: The Doer

Core desire: To be valuable, admired, and influential
Core fear: Being exposed, humiliated, and unadmired

Enneagram 3s are not just achievers—they are people who hold the capacity for amazing generosity and compassion. They can be the best team player you know when they are healthy, making space for vulnerability along with efficiency. Until they believe this vulnerability won't cost them their appearance or status, however, they can exchange connection for something shallow. This can be a slippery slope, leading to 3s avoiding what vulnerable, authentic connection has to offer. There is a lack of freedom and heightened anxiety with Enneagram 3s. Constantly being on the lookout for ways to relate, ways to impress, or even ways to simply blend in can be exhausting. Enneagram 3s crave acceptance in general, even if it means sacrificing their true selves. Enneagram 3s grow, however, when they begin to notice their subconscious patterns and embrace the anxiety. Maybe desiring acceptance as your true self is a beautifully normal, human thing?

Enneagram 4: The Seeker

Core desire: To be accepted and to discover what makes them significant
Core fear: Being without a distinct identity, having no personal significance, meaninglessness

Enneagram 4s are not just romantics—they can be quite balanced and practical when in good health. They desire to feel a sense of identity and significance in the world, but they also show great objectivity when it is necessary. This doesn't always look like purposefully standing out from the crowd—in fact, many Enneagram 4s have said that isn't what they want. They are acutely aware of how they are being perceived. And though they would like to be different and significant in some ways, for the most part, they want to feel a sense of similarity with others as opposed to otherness. Until they believe they will be rescued from this inner turmoil, however, they can exchange their authentic relationships for imaginary ones. Enneagram 4s have a rich internal world that can often be more pleasant to reside in than the one around them, longing for true community by imagining how they would like to be in it. For many 4s, this can cause them to not only isolate themselves, but to remain in a push-pull cycle with the people they love. One second, they are all in, all present—the next, they may seem to just disappear. The disappearance usually comes from insecurity or feeling the effects of how this internal world they've built is better than the one they are living in.

Enneagram 5: The Investigator

Core desire: To be self-reliant, competent, capable, and useful
Core fear: Being useless, dependent, helpless, and depleted

Enneagram 5s are not just investigators—they are wildly passionate and coura-geous when in good health. They can be the most forthright, assertive folks you know, allowing their wisdom to influence them into solid action. But this can be hard for them to step into if they do not feel like they are capable or competent. Enneagram 5s naturally enjoy both the presence of real community and alone time. Even extroverted 5s cannot replace or replicate the value they place on spending time alone and how precious it is to them. If their relationship with their alone time is excessive or in an unhealthy place, this can also lead them to isolate themselves from others like Enneagram 4s. This isn't always retreating into an internal world, but simply beginning to believe they don't need others to survive since they do it so well on their own.

Enneagram 6: The Advocate

Core desire: To be supported and guided, and to have a maintained sense of belonging

Core fear: Being unsafe, unstable, and without security

Enneagram 6s are not just questioners—they also prioritize peace and coziness. Perhaps they love their morning routines or morning coffee—they consider the small things to be sacred. They can be loving and accepting, but this easygoing nature can be hard for them to tap into if they do not feel as though they are secure. Belonging and a sense of security are what they prioritize and look for when it comes to community. When they feel as though they cannot fully rely on a person or group of people, when they feel as though their concerns and questions are not welcome, they become suspicious. This suspiciousness can either cause them to rebel against the community they are pursuing, or to overly submit to it.

Enneagram 7: The Explorer

Core desire: To be fulfilled, unlimited, and taken care of
Core fear: Being deprived of opportunity or adventure, being trapped or
stuck in pain

Enneagram 7s are not just enthusiasts—they can also be serene and rooted when they are in good health. A lot of 7s enjoy a slow pace of living, delighting in all that the present has to offer them. But this can be hard for them to live out when they begin to feel trapped. Feeling trapped is one of Enneagram 7s' core fears and motivators; it is why many of them revert to escapism and avoidance. Some ways 7s can begin to feel stuck or trapped are through conversations that go too far and communities that feel too smothering. When they feel as though people are beginning to expect a lot from them, or they have volunteered themselves and their time one too many times, it can be easy for them to just bail. Like 4s, 7s can struggle with a push-pull cycle, but motivation has less to do with insecurity and more to do with suppressed feelings—whether that means beginning to feel trapped, feeling too much like the class clown, feeling that who they are is too much, etc.

Enneagram 8: The Defender

Core desire: To be strong, to be a pioneer for their own life and destiny
Core fear: Being at the mercy or in the grip of power of another, being harmed
   or taken advantage of

Enneagram 8s are not just challengers—they can be incredibly tenderhearted and helpful. Many Enneagram 8s protect their loved ones with their time, energy, resources, etc. They find a lot of joy in that protection. However, their tenderheartedness can be hard to access if they start to sense betrayal. Betrayal for an Enneagram 8 can look like many different things: someone betraying beliefs they thought were mutually agreed upon, betrayal to not hash things out, betrayal to a system or cause or person they hold dear. It could even be the past or a dreamed future. The line of betrayal quickly crosses into disappointment, which can lead Enneagram 8s to become very angry. 8s do not enjoy conflict, but they are not afraid of it like a lot of the other types on the Enneagram. They believe that conflict is a part of life, and it should be talked about and resolved— whether or not someone else wants to resolve it. Enneagram 8s may also enjoy a little battle every now and again.

Enneagram 9: The Peacemaker

Core desire: To be unaffected, at peace, and interconnected
Core fear: Being cut off from love, or experiencing loss and separation from someone or something

Enneagram 9s are not just peacemakers, but also charismatic individuals who act on what they believe in. They are leaders, speakers, teachers, and more. However, it is difficult for them to step into this role naturally if they sense there will be disconnection or potential separation from those they love. This is why many Peacemakers often earn a reputation for being more quiet or easygoing individuals. The amount of worry that Peacemakers feel regarding disconnection is sizable, and they work to maintain internal and relational peace at all costs. In fact, many Peacemakers have the hardest time identifying themselves within the Enneagram personality system because of the parts of others they've picked up within themselves throughout life. Amazing mediators and chameleons, Peacemakers, like other types, find that their greatest strength is also their Achilles' heel.

Levels of Health

An important aspect of the Enneagram personality system that will help you understand the complexities not only of yourself, but of others, is the Levels of Health for each Enneagram number. Though the Enneagram is not the gospel, and it does not explain the intricacies of human personality, the Levels of Health add dimension to the typical Enneagram number and core desires. Throughout each chapter, I will be using the Levels of Health to discuss how each Enneagram type may appear as a friend during times of . . .

- Health
- Coasting
- Stress

Level 1: Health

As you would assume, the first level within the Levels of Health is Health. What "health" means in this case is that you are in a state of being self-actualized. Though you still struggle with your core desires and fears, you understand how they influence your behavior in the world. You are self-aware and working toward compassion for yourself and others. You are working to heal the parts of you that have been wounded, and you are dedicated to seeing beyond yourself in friendships and relationships. You may still wrestle with the same harmful narrative as before, but it does not leave you falling apart. For all Enneagram types, living in a healthier state of being will result in you exhibiting positive traits of another Enneagram number. This breaks down as follows . . .

- Enneagram 1 (The Improver) may seem like a balanced Enneagram 7 (The Explorer) in Health
- Enneagram 2 (The Giver) may seem like a balanced Enneagram 4 (The Seeker) in Health

- Enneagram 3 (The Doer) may seem like a balanced Enneagram 6 (The Advocate) in Health
- Enneagram 4 (The Seeker) may seem like a balanced Enneagram 1 (The Improver) in Health
- Enneagram 5 (The Investigator) may seem like a balanced Enneagram 8 (The Defender) in Health
- Enneagram 6 (The Advocate) may seem like a balanced Enneagram 9 (The Peacemaker) in Health
- Enneagram 7 (The Explorer) may seem like a balanced Enneagram 5 (The Investigator) in Health
- Enneagram 8 (The Defender) may seem like a balanced Enneagram 2 (The Giver) in Health
- Enneagram 9 (The Peacemaker) may seem like a balanced Enneagram 3 (The Doer) in Health

Level 2: Coasting

When Levels of Health are talked about regarding the Enneagram, the state in-between Health and Stress isn't usually labeled because it seems obvious. If it is discussed, this state of being is called "Average." You're not on your A game, but you're not in distress. I have decided to call this in-between and the reality of where most of us exist most of the time "Coasting." We may not be making efforts to become more self-aware, but we are at least aware of our general tendencies. We may not be in therapy, but we're reading a book about the Enneagram! We're not spiraling into a pit of despair—we're simply here. We are existing, processing, maybe even enjoying life. Multiple times throughout this book, I mention that the "Coasting" state is when your more stereotypical Enneagram type qualities are prevalent, and it will be easiest to identify your Enneagram number.

Level 3: Stress

To understand the full scope of the Levels of Health, we must dive into the idea of Stress for each Enneagram number. Many Enneagram teachers prefer to refer to this state as "Resource" instead of "Stress" because it is meant to describe how we feel when we are grasping at straws or gasping for air during the throes of life. It means we are going beyond our internal means to satisfy longing, to cope with pain, or to quite literally survive the circumstances in front of us. Everyone gets stressed from time to time. But each Enneagram type takes on specific qualities when they find themselves in a residual state of stress or cyclical behavioral unhealthiness.

- Enneagram 1 (The Improver) may seem like a Coasting or Stressed Enneagram 4 (The Seeker)
- Enneagram 2 (The Giver) may seem like a Coasting or Stressed Enneagram 8 (The Defender)
- Enneagram 3 (The Doer) may seem like a Coasting or Stressed Enneagram 9 (The Peacemaker)
- Enneagram 4 (The Seeker) may seem like a Coasting or Stressed Enneagram 2 (The Giver)
- Enneagram 5 (The Investigator) may seem like a Coasting or Stressed Enneagram 7 (The Explorer)
- Enneagram 6 (The Advocate) may seem like a Coasting or Stressed Enneagram 3 (The Doer)
- Enneagram 7 (The Explorer) may seem like a Coasting or Stressed Enneagram 1 (The Improver)
- Enneagram 8 (The Defender) may seem like a Coasting or Stressed Enneagram 5 (The Investigator)
- Enneagram 9 (The Peacemaker) may seem like a Coasting or Stressed Enneagram 6 (The Advocate)

The Levels of Health not only help us go beyond our core desires and fears, but when viewed in the light of interpersonal relationships, you can easily see how each personality could become activated by another. There are as many recipes for harmony as there are for disaster, and I personally believe that someone's Level of Health has more to do with compatibility than their number pairing.

Understanding Enneagram Triads

To understand your individual number, it is helpful to recognize which Enneagram Triad you are in. There are three Enneagram Triads that help determine key motivating factors of a person's behavior. These Triads are broken down into how you experience emotion, stress, and event processing.

The three Enneagram Triads are . . .

- The Heart Triad (2, 3, & 4)
- The Mind Triad (5, 6, & 7)
- The Gut Triad (1, 8, & 9)

The Heart Triad

The Heart Triad is made up of Enneagram 2 (The Giver), Enneagram 3 (The Doer), and Enneagram 4 (The Seeker). These three types are said to be in the Heart Triad because they process experiences and emotions through feelings first. Givers, Enneagram 2s, absorb the emotional experiences of others around them like a sponge. Because Givers are so inclined to lead with their heart, they can often feel a sense of entrapment in the swirl of emotional chaos. Similarly, Seekers, Enneagram 4s, grapple with this balance of empathy but on a more internal level. Seekers are in the Heart Triad because they tend to over-identify with their emotional experience. Where Givers may be inspired to help others when confronted with a painful emotional experience, Seekers are often inspired to understand them and relate it back to their own personal experience. Seekers are subconsciously looking to find themselves in another's experience, to both relate and feel a sense of connection. This gets sticky when this initial desire to understand morphs into emotional projection. Most Doers (Enneagram 3s) do not see themselves as emotional people. Doers, however, are in the Heart Triad because they wrestle the most with suppressed emotions. Many Doers feel very deeply, but with the combination of their nature and their nurture, they have become people who believe that their emotional experience is attached to a long list of what they should or shouldn't feel. In summary, Givers externalize their emotional experience, Seekers internalize their emotional experience, and Doers mask their emotional experience.

The Mind Triad

The Mind Triad is made up of Enneagram 5 (The Investigator), Enneagram 6 (The Advocate), and Enneagram 7 (The Explorer). These three types are placed in the Mind Triad because they tend to over- or under-intellectualize their stressors and emotional experiences. They seek to process, not necessarily through logic but inside their stream of consciousness. All three Mind types may feel disconnected from their emotions or their gut due to their constant mental stimulation. For Investigators, Enneagram 5s, mental processing tends to lean more toward the overthinking category. This does not simply involve worrying or having anxious thoughts but instead involves analyzing themselves and others to the point of exhaustion. Investigators can feel as though their thoughts and process of analysis are an endless well that reaches no bottom, succumbing to the belief that they will finally be capable and competent when they find the answer they're looking for. Enneagram 7s, Explorers, are prone to the under-thinking struggle. Though their minds are incredibly active and curious, the constant stream of thoughts keeps their emotions and gut feelings at bay. It may not seem as though they are in the Mind Triad on the outside because of how much they are moving and expressing outwardly, but their mind is the main thing protecting them from feeling any displeasure. Like Doers in the Heart Triad, Enneagram 6s, Advocates, are in the Mind Triad despite being disconnected to their thought process. Many Advocates out there may think that they're "thinking all the time," but that does not equal being mindful of how their thought patterns are derailing or changing. Advocates can also become captive to their thought spirals, leaving them feeling numb or paralyzed.

The Gut Triad

Lastly, the Gut Triad is made up of Enneagram 1 (The Improver), Enneagram 8 (The Defender), and Enneagram 9 (The Peacemaker). These types are in the Gut Triad because they tend to process their experiences and emotions through physical sensations, mainly feeling anger or frustration or the suppression of anger and frustration before anything else. Enneagram 1s, Improvers, are in the Gut Triad because of the boiling sense of justice and resentment they simultaneously suppress and express. Many Improvers struggle because of their belief that anger is inherently bad, which is why they redirect most of their frustration toward themselves internally. Enneagram 8s, Defenders, are in the Gut Triad because they tend to boldly express their anger and frustration outwardly. Defenders may feel like the only emotion they experience is anger, but that is not true. Underneath the anger, they feel very deeply, and they use their anger to suppress the other emotions they are experiencing. Enneagram 9, The Peacemaker, is in the same camp as Doers and Defenders. Though they are in the Gut Triad because they feel things primarily in their gut, that also happens to be the part of themselves they are most disconnected from. Peacemakers believe, similarly to Improvers, that the feeling and expression of anger is inherently bad. Peacemakers, however, also believe that anger or conflict can directly affect their peace, which is why they are the most disconnected from their anger of all the Enneagram types.

Understanding Enneagram Stances

As we continue to get to know the Enneagram types, it is important to learn each Enneagram number's Stance on how they interact with the world. This also can be explained in three different groupings.

- The Assertive Stance (Enneagram 3, 7, & 8)
- The Dutiful Stance (Enneagram 1, 2, & 6)
- The Withdrawing Stance (Enneagram 4, 5 & 9)

The Assertive Stance

The Assertive Stance is made up of Enneagram 3 (The Doer), Enneagram 7 (The Explorer), and Enneagram 8 (The Defender). When I refer to these types as Assertive, it simply means that their approach to the world is to move toward it: to focus on the future, where they need to go, who they need to meet. Even when introverted, they tend to go about the world in a bold way, unafraid to go after what they desire in life. Though this is an admirable quality for the Assertive types, it does mean they tend to struggle with remaining present in their life and taking the time to take care of their current needs or past experiences.

The Dutiful Stance

The Dutiful Stance holds Enneagram 1 (The Improver), Enneagram 2 (The Giver), and Enneagram 6 (The Advocate). Where the Assertive Stance goes toward the world, these three types instead feel an obligation to the world. Improvers, Givers, and Advocates may feel as though they are wired to make an impact and help those in need. They move with others and find great fulfillment in the responsibility they feel toward making the world and others better. This quality in the Dutiful Stance truly keeps our world running, but it also leaves these three types susceptible to remaining hyper-focused on the present. Sometimes these types can suppress the past or worry about future outcomes because of the magnitude of the unknown. This can lead them to have poor self-care when they are unhealthy, leading to poor physical and emotional hygiene if they are not careful.

The Withdrawn Stance

Enneagram 4 (The Seeker), Enneagram 5 (The Investigator), and Enneagram 9 (The Peacemaker) all make up the Withdrawn Stance. While the Assertive Stance moves toward the world and the Dutiful Stance feels responsibility for the world, the types in the Withdrawn Stance may find themselves withdrawing from the world, whether into their internal world, their thoughts, or working to maintain their inner peace. While Seekers, Investigators, and Peacemakers are still helpful and ambitious people, they tend naturally toward reflection and contemplation. These types may feel as though the world is too much or too invasive at times, and they find joy and solitude in retreating toward themselves. Though the ability to find and remain connected to one's internal world is important, this can lead to a dismissal or avoidance of both the present and the future for the Withdrawn Stance.

Understanding Enneagram Conflict Styles

The final grouping of Enneagram types I will reference throughout this book pertains to each Enneagram number's conflict style. Each type not only has a way of processing emotions and a way of approaching the world, but they also tend to deal with emotions in the midst of friction. These groupings can be broken down as follows . . .

- Reactivity (Enneagram 4, 6, & 8)
- Optimism (Enneagram 2, 7, & 9)
- Logic (Enneagram 1, 3, & 5)

Reactivity

Enneagram 4 (The Seeker), Enneagram 6 (The Advocate), and Enneagram 8 (The Defender) find themselves in the Reactivity group when it comes to conflict because they all tend to react first and process second. This means that Seekers may react through expressing how they feel, Advocates may react through distrust and questioning, and Defenders may react with frustration or anger. The strength of the Reactivity group is that they are mostly unafraid of expressing themselves and their concerns; the fault is when their reactions override how they truly feel about the situation. It is important for Seekers, Advocates, and Defenders to be aware of their reactivity and for others to understand that these three types do have feelings underneath those reactions, but they may need some patience before they will share.

Optimism

The Optimism group is filled with Enneagram 2 (The Giver), Enneagram 7 (The Explorer), and Enneagram 9 (The Peacemaker). When these three types find themselves in conflict, they tend to take a positive outlook, working to appease others' emotional responses either through agreement or avoidance. Givers will work to appease the conflict by going into service or control mode, Explorers will work to find the bright side and a vision for the future, and Peacemakers either avoid or agree amid the tension in order to not disrupt any relational peace that could be possible. It is admirable how these three types face difficult relational conflicts with such positivity, but it also can keep them from emotional honesty and follow-through. It is important for these types to remember that though pain is painful, it is necessary for healing to take place. Others may need to reassure them that they are still loved and things will still be great through it all.

Logic

To - Do
☑ Be better
☑ Do better
☑ Look better

Enneagram 1 (The Improver), Enneagram 3 (The Doer), and Enneagram 5 (The Investigator) are all in the Logic group of processing conflict. This means that before understanding their emotions toward a situation, they will often process with rationale. Improvers will work to critique and find the right solution, Doers will work to self-preserve and plan for the future, and Investigators will work to dissect and understand the conflict in its entirety. Though this approach may seem like it is the most logical, just like in the other groupings, the true feelings of each of these types lies underneath their precise approach. It is important for those in the Logic group to stay aware of their detachment or coldness in conflicts, and it is important for others to remember that processing with logic is often a coping mechanism to feel better about what they are experiencing.

Focusing on ourselves to become better friends is a key aspect of growth, but in this movement of self-improvement, we can forget how serving others and being kind also are necessary for growth. For us to reach the relationship goals we desire, we must be willing to sacrifice in some way. This is not a call to abandon or sacrifice yourself, but it is a call to humility. Friendship, regardless of Enneagram type, is impossible without a commitment to humility.

In my previous book, *Take Care of Your Type*, the emphasis and overall theme pertained to self-care. The hard work to make sure you are taking good care of your well-being and soul goes beyond taking more baths and eating cleaner. In this book, I want to invite you into a space where you can care deeply for others. Friendship-care, we can call it. This is a place where you can let your guard down and be vulnerable to yourself and others. To look in the mirror and see how you contribute to your friendships, both positively and negatively. No matter how we slice it, we do affect other people, and though we don't have to carry that responsibility, it is good to be aware of it. I am sick of living in a black and white world where you are either taking good care of yourself or taking good care of others—never both at the same time. I believe both can be possible; it just takes work. I hope that work becomes appealing after diving into the themes of this book.

The Six Pillars of Friendship

An article published by *The Atlantic* in 2021 serves as a large portion of the inspiration for this book. As we make sense of the aftermath of the pandemic, I think many people have realized the importance of community and how lonely we actually feel. More than physical isolation, the emotional and socioeconomic wreckage have taken a toll on us. I wanted to write a book using the Enneagram that would not only be applicable to our lives beyond these years of repairing, but hopefully as something that could be used as a tool in the process. When I started researching for this book, I came across *The Friendship Files* series from *The Atlantic* and immediately dove in deep. The article that stuck out to me the most discussed the "Six Pillars of Friendship," outlined as follows . . .

- Accessibility

The art of being accessible starts with putting yourself in the way of potential friendship, whether that be through extracurricular activities in person or online, participating in group chats or conversations, etc. The art of accessibility also comes into play by being open and vulnerable to emotional connection.

- Attention

Friends can be where you least expect them. In order to maintain friendships, you not only need to pay attention to their cares and worries, but also to where they physically are around you in your life. Making yourself accessible means you have to pay attention!

- Intention

In this book, I will discuss why it might be hard for you to be intentional based on your type, and why intentionality is necessary for a successful friendship. Without taking the time to pursue friendships purposefully, it will be hard to sustain connections.

- Habit

Habits in friendship look like meeting every week, month, or year. It could also mean sticking to a promise to stay in contact through calls, vacations, or coffee dates. Creating rituals in your friendships ultimately determines their longevity.

- Imagination

No, I'm not referencing imaginary friends. It is important to change your perspective when it comes to friendship. Try to imagine what kind of friend you could be and who you want to connect with in your life. What you want versus what you need may be drastically different. Take risks in the activities you do together, and take risks in who you are intentional with. You may be surprised!

- Grace

Every relationship needs a level of grace and forgiveness to stay connected, especially in adult friendships. No one is perfect, and learning healthy communication skills and learning from your mistakes will foster deeper connections that can last a lifetime!

Throughout the tips in this book, I will refer to these pillars often, as I believe that discoveries found in this research are incredibly valuable when applied to our interpersonal relationships!

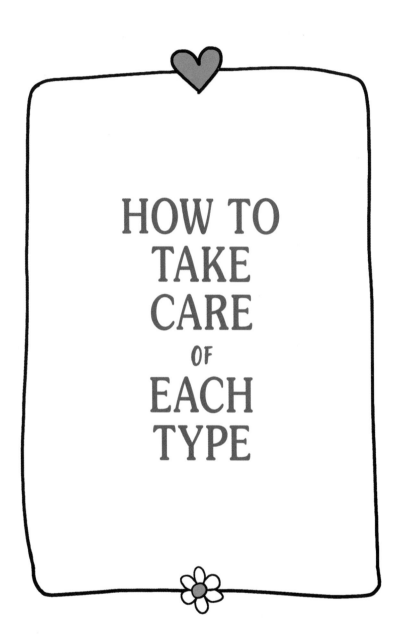

HOW TO
TAKE
CARE
OF
EACH
TYPE

ENNEAGRAM 1

Introduction

Enneagram 1s, commonly known as the Improver or Reformer, are individuals who desire what is good and to be good as they define it above all else. They typically value integrity and accuracy, working to be above reproach and beyond condemnation from others in everything they do. They fear becoming corrupted or tainted by beliefs that don't align with their own. Though they are usually painted as rule-followers, they can also be rule-breakers if they do not believe that the rules in place are up to their standards. Improvers have an incessant inner critic that assaults them with mistakes, judgments, and critiques directed toward themselves and others. In light of these qualities, Improvers are also incredibly kind and wise people who can extend profound compassion and insight to those who are loved by them.

Improvers as a Friend when Healthy

When Improvers are Healthy, they emulate many qualities that are like an Explorer on the Enneagram. Though they still value their convictions, they can prioritize both pleasure and responsibility in their lives They understand that true balance comes from enjoying life as well as carrying the burden of it. Improvers become more open-minded, choosing to accept that not everything is black-and-white. They may not be fully comfortable in the gray areas, but they see the importance of accepting them. Speaking of accepting, nonjudgmental feedback also comes easier to Improvers when they are in a Healthy state of being. They understand that emotional intelligence and rationality go together when it comes to their relationships. Improvers begin to show up in their life rawer, allowing their creativity and expression to flow. They see the beauty in the unrefined and the unreconciled, becoming a powerful force of joy and reconciliation in the lives of those they love. Improvers will be there for you in practical and supportive ways, stealing you for adventures and fun excursions and being thoughtful in their relational approach. They will be slower to criticize and quicker to apologize, honoring and cherishing you deeply.

Improvers as a Friend when Coasting

I consider Improvers to be humorous individuals when they are Coasting. They will begin to open up their goofy side to you as they become more comfortable while also being less hesitant to share their criticisms. They will still be very insightful people, providing sound advice in most situations. However, they also will be more prone to ranting as a way to communicate their true feelings. They will be quicker to criticize and will have a harder time seeing your side of things. When they are not actively working toward being healthier, many Improvers tend to die on their hill of rightness; it will take them much longer to reach a point of compromise. While they will be quick to criticize others, they will be unable to receive criticism from anyone else. You would think that their ability to make harsh judgments would lead to thicker skin, but Improvers are just as sensitive as the rest of us. Because of their inner critic, Improvers may have a blind spot to how they project that inner critic onto others when they are simply Coasting.

Improvers as a Friend when Stressed

Typically dutiful and active, Improvers suddenly become even more hypercritical and withdrawn. They can feel trapped inside their internal world, imagining how anyone else but them would be able to be better at life than them, how someone else could magically become the better version of themselves that they're striving to be. Improvers will feel misunderstood by those around them and simultaneously become more rigid in their ideals and more avoidant of responsibility.

Taking Care of an Improver

Tip #1: *Avoid demanding an emotional response*

Contrary to many Improver stereotypes, I believe that Improvers can be very in touch with their emotions. Though they may not always be quick to understand, I've seen most of the Improvers in my life be quick to sympathize when they care about the person who is struggling. In friendships or relationships, however, it is imperative to remember that an outward show of emotions is not always comfortable for Improvers. This does not mean they are not sympathizing or experiencing emotions; in fact, their desire to improve your situation is one way they process their internal feelings. This means that your expected emotional response from them in moments of grief, panic, sadness, change, celebration, etc., may not be what you receive in the moment. Though this can be disappointing for Enneagram personalities who are more apt to expressing their feelings in the moment, the worst thing you can do to an Improver in these scenarios is demand an emotional response from them. Demanding an emotional response from an Improver before they are ready dismantles the potential feeling of security that could be developed when allowing them to process things at their own pace. Though it may be inconvenient for you, you must remember that emotional expression does not operate on a scale of convenience, but safety.

Tip #2: *Their inner critic is also against them*

Improvers within the Enneagram personality system are also known for being rather critical individuals. When most people think of an Enneagram 1, they think of someone who is extremely judgmental or nitpicky. While this can be true when Improvers are in an unhealthy behavioral cycle, it is important to remember that their usual slight jabs or critical observations are voiced because they are suffering from a critical voice within them. According to Beth McCord, founder of The Enneagram Coach, Improvers point out mistakes because any form of error or mistake assaults their mind against their will. Most Improvers would prefer not to be plagued with the constant mental fatigue of noticing things that they consider to be wrong, but it happens mostly subconsciously. In fact, many Improvers may not realize they have an inner critic until they read about Improvers having an inner critic. It usually is a big light-bulb moment for them.

Tip #3: *Show integrity in your support*

My friend and I were talking over paper plates filled with fruit, dips, and cookies. I had chosen to grab watermelon, which was a different choice for me, and found myself enjoying both my expanding fruit palate and my friend's conversation. This particular friend of mine is one of those people that you know would have the highest IQ out of your friend group. She's a fantasy reader, accountant, and diligent presence in everyone's life. She is also incredibly creative but has difficulty leaning into that creative side without feeling guilty. This was our topic of conversation. She is at a place in her job where her tasks run like a well-oiled machine. They feel like second nature to her at this point, and she has found herself with a lot of extra time on her hands throughout the day–time she spends making board games in Canva, watching YouTube videos, playing chess, etc. I suggested that she should start writing scripts for the podcast she's been dreaming of starting during that time. She immediately expressed that is what she genuinely likes to do, but that she finds herself spiraling into a battle of internal integrity. Watching YouTube feels less risky than working on a project of her own during work hours, even if she has nothing else to do at work.

This internal battle of integrity across a plethora of scenarios is a trademark trait of Improvers. They fear external condemnation as much as they fear their own inner critic's condemnation, which is why many of the Improvers you know, regardless of their level of health, are people who hold firm to their beliefs about right and wrong. When showing support to the Improver in your life, it is important that you are aware of this battle of integrity, because they automatically expect that you feel the same pressure as they do when it comes to offering help, showing up for the people in their life, and meaning what they say. Embrace honesty and truth in love in ways that may feel uncomfortable for you but are helpful for an Improver. Not in a way that changes who you are, but as an act of compromise and servitude. If you say you will show up, say it and mean it. If you say you want to help, show up and help. If you want to share your truth with them, share it regardless of whether you think they will become upset. Improvers respect this level of authenticity, even if it is uncomfortable for them as well.

Tip #4: *Help carry the weight*

When I first started posting about the Enneagram online, I was struck by a mental depiction I imagined of an Improver one evening. For some reason, I always envision Greek mythology when I think of Improvers. The battles, the marble, the fables . . . it all gives very Type 1 energy.

Improvers bear a unique burden and weight of the world. They strive for goodness within themselves, but also strive for goodness in the world. They are born with an innate sense of seeing how we could be better humans; it's a remarkable gift and an exhausting burden, especially when it feels like you are the only one who cares so deeply about the goodness of the world. Though Improvers want to share this burden with others, deep down, they do not know how to express their desire to have someone lighten the weight on their shoulders. This is why it is important as a friend, loved one, or partner of an Improver to become intuitive to the effect of this burdensome grief on your Improver. Acknowledge it, even if you are afraid that you don't have the right words. What is a small piece of the world that you can take off of their plate? Maybe it is as simple as a chore around the house, but maybe it could be learning about a topic your Improver is passionate about. It could even be as approachable as acknowledging the burden they are carrying without them having to bring it up. Seeking to understand without relying on the Improver to help you understand it would mean the world to many Improvers. Show genuine interest. Give verbal affirmation. Let your Improver accept a hug and a moment of relaxation on the couch for the night.

Tip #5: *Encourage enjoyment*

If you know an Improver, you know that they have quite the adventure-seeking, goofy-goober side to them. They are witty and can even have a dark, outlandish, secret sense of humor. They love the finer things in life and often crave self-indulgence. In fact, some Improvers crave self-indulgence so deeply they will become more rigid with themselves so that they do not step out of line with their ideals. Or they might build an internal reward system that reinforces a belief that they are only deserving of self-indulgence when they've earned it. As the friend or partner of an Improver, encourage them to enjoy themselves regardless of whether they feel they've earned it. Desiring comfort and items of quality does not discount their fervor or convictions. Humans are allowed to exist complexly, which includes affording themselves the balance of letting loose and staying grounded.

Becoming a Better Friend as an Improver

Tip #1: *Is it bettering or berating?*

As I was talking with one of my dear Improver friends about the themes for this book, I realized how Improvers have the desire for growth written in their DNA. Every decision, every piece of advice, every observation they make about themselves, others, and the world is through the lens of: "How can this be better?"

The advice that they give comes from a genuine desire to see their friend or loved one improve. As my Improver friend and I were talking, she and I both realized simultaneously that one of her blind spots is not realizing what she is expressing is criticism. Because Improvers have such a constant harsh inner critic, they almost become numb to what criticism sounds like. Though Improvers eventually realize that they have an inner critic, they assume that the voice bullying them into constant growth is a voice that everyone has inside them—that the inner critic's voice is one for the betterment of themselves or others, when in reality, this voice is berating and unruly. It may appear to be motivated by a sacred moral compass, but it is actually motivated by an Improver's core fear: being tainted, condemned, and without integrity.

Many Improvers have a hard time recognizing their outward criticism of others, because to them it does not feel like criticism—it feels like help. It feels like growth, possibly because that is all they've ever known in the clutches of the inner critic. This is why the first step for a Type 1 on the Enneagram who wants to become a better friend is to become a better friend to themselves. Uncovering your inner supporter is not easy, and it will look different for every Improver. It may require therapy or acquiring a self-reflective habit of some kind. It does not mean allowing your mind to bully you into behaviors that you think are more correct than the ones you are doing now. It means taking steps toward healing and forgiving all of the distorted ways your inner critic tries to protect you from your worst fears. This means understanding that perhaps this berating voice is not one that serves you but is the voice of an anxious inner child. The more you simultaneously ignore the core fears and emotions while honoring the voice of your inner critic, the more you prolong the process of experiencing authentic, long-lasting growth, both inside you and within your relationships.

Tip #2: *The distraction of growth*

I'm sure if you talk with any Improver, you will quickly find how oriented toward growth they are as individuals. This can be growth in relation to work goals, family milestones, or even reaching spiritual or mental heights. Growth is more than just something they work toward or dream about; it is written in their DNA. One of the many ways Improvers take stock of their interpersonal relationships is how much they feel like those relationships help them or the other person improve. Though this is an important aspect of relationships, it de-normalizes the mundane, stagnant parts that are naturally a part of most relationships and friendships. If there is always growth, there may not be peace or rest. Because growth is ranked as the higher priority above some of the more indulgent aspects of relationships for Improvers, this can cause them to become hyper-critical of themselves or their loved one. It can even cause an Improver to leave a healthy relationship or friendship behind if it is not measuring up to the ideal trajectory of growth the Improver had in mind for it.

This means becoming a better friend and partner as an Improver in this aspect of interpersonal relationships is realizing that perhaps growth is healthy, but the endless, continual pursuit of it above all else is not. In fact, the hyper-focus on growth can end up being a distraction from what is already good, true, and lovely in your friendships. An Improver can go about reorienting their mind to focus on more than just growth by allowing their priorities to take turns. Let growth take a seat in order for joy to stand up! Let joy take a seat in order for disappointment or sadness to process. Allow your focus to become more well-rounded as opposed to one-sided. You may find that growth is going at a slower pace than usual, but it is far more rich and satisfying in the long run.

Tip #3: *Meet amid imperfection*

If I could have it my way, I would have a very specific and warm routine for how I write this book. I've had incredibly high standards for how my pen meets the paper or my fingers meet the keyboard, none of which have gone according to plan in the end. When my husband and I were finally going to decorate our home office, we had finally purchased the walking pad for my standing desk when our basement, where our office resided, flooded. My dream of writing my next book in a nook-like corner of our home where I could pretend that I was a student at Oxford was washed away with the hazardous summer rain. Rather than adapting quickly to this obstacle, I let it impact how much writing I get done. If it cannot be done perfectly and just right, then I have to wait for those conditions to get started. This has obviously set me back quite a bit, and I am not approaching my manuscript deadline in a panic as I roll my eyes at the cycle I have taken part in again.

Many Improvers can relate to this feeling, not just in terms of their own projects but in their relationships as well. Say you finally found someone you wanted to commit to, whether romantically or in friendship. Things are going extremely well . . . until the inner critic chimes in.

"You're moving too fast," "You're moving too slow," "You haven't fought enough," "You are fighting too much," "This is not how you fully envisioned this relationship," "That was a silly mistake they made," "I hope I can teach them the right way to do this," etc.

The truth is, if you want to experience an idealistic relationship, you're going to have to practice the acceptance of change, error, and setbacks that are natural and healthy. Practice viewing the world in a way where, yes, you may be noticing things that are "wrong," but you can move forward despite them. You can discern the cost of pointing it out without the existential crisis and weight of figuring it all out. Practice patience toward what you consider to be filled with flaws, and build the courage to move forward anyway.

Tip #4: *Lean into the support of others*

On a more practical note, many Improvers may struggle to gather with those they love when the settings are not as perfect as they envisioned. Maybe it's because their house isn't what they have in mind yet, or the friend group they're trying to form isn't what they've imagined yet. I want to encourage Improvers by noting that your relationships desire more from you than your ability to show up and show out perfectly, and that should be a huge relief. That aesthetically pleasing movie night that you're romanticizing? Plan it! Plan it in the house or room you have access to at the moment. If this isn't possible for you, see if someone else will host and you can support them by organizing the snacks. Let go of the reins and allow yourself to enjoy your friendships where they are, as they are, today.

Tip #5: *Extend grace over evaluation*

In my first job right out of college, it became clear quickly that the two bosses I was working for and I were not going to get along long term. I denied this fact for months because of how much I desired to please them and make it work, but it seemed as though no matter how many hoops I jumped through and tricks I performed for them, there was always something wrong that I could be doing better. I found out toward the end of my time in this workplace that one of my bosses identified as an Improver. She began to use language in relation to the Enneagram to excuse a lot of her managerial behavior toward me, as opposed to using the Enneagram as a tool of self-awareness. In fact, when she found out my Enneagram type, she asked me how my Enneagram type could become more like hers.

This is a very extreme case with an unhealthy Improver, and I know from more personal experience that not all Improvers operate this way externally. However, I do believe what my boss was experiencing is a common internal tension Improvers feel entrapped in. They want to extend grace, but how can they extend grace when they do not consider themselves worthy of grace at all? An Improver may even think, "If I am striving so hard to be good and worthy, others should, too." The funny thing about grace is that in its very definition, it is not something that is earned, but bestowed. And for an Improver to learn how to give grace to others, they must learn to accept the gift of grace for themselves. There is no striving that can be done that makes you more worthy of goodness or earns you more integrity.

What if others are not truly honoring you by bending over backward to meet your expectations? What if you are not being loving or helpful toward yourself by forcing yourself to contort in all the ways you think others should too? I want to invite you, as an Improver, or the Improver you're thinking of as you read this, into a space of grace upon grace upon grace upon grace upon grace. Where it doesn't run out because it can't. It is an overflowing stream, a rushing river that is waiting for you to dance in. Join the dance of grace and bring others along with you!

Approaching Conflict with an Improver

You may experience conflict with an Improver because . . .
- If you are a fellow Improver, you have different convictions of right and wrong
- If you are a Giver, they seem to put truth and order before love
- If you are a Doer, they seem like nothing is good enough for them
- If you are a Seeker, they seem like they want to fix you
- If you are an Investigator, they seem to care only about convictions regardless of facts
- If you are an Advocate, they seem to value rightness more than what is best for the common good
- If you are an Explorer, they seem like they're judging you for your excitement and optimism
- If you are a Defender, they seem to have different beliefs regarding justice
- If you are a Peacemaker, they seem like they are trying to dominate your decisions

As an Improver, you may experience conflict . . .
- With a fellow Improver, because you have opposing views of perfection
- With a Giver, because they seem to base their values solely on the values of others

- With a Doer, because they seem to care more about being the best as opposed to being correct
- With a Seeker, because they seem to only care about what they feel as opposed to what is
- With an Investigator, because they seem to always need a reason why
- With an Advocate, because their process of overthinking clashes with yours
- With an Explorer, because they seem to be your polar opposite
- With a Defender, because they tend to dismiss and dominate
- With a Peacemaker, because they seem to always need guidance

We can't control the behavior of others, BUT here is what you can do . . .
- Have empathy for the shared experience of an inner critic (1)
- Understand that holding the values of others as important increases connection and respect in a relationship (2)
- Remember things aren't always black and white. Sometimes progress is needed over perfection! (3)
- Learn that emotionality is a valuable part of processing information and experiences (4)
- Try replacing defensiveness with curiosity (5)
- Understand that seeking guidance from others doesn't mean you lack conviction (6)
- Remember that just because your life works for you doesn't mean it'll work for someone else (7)
- Learn to express honestly without expressing criticism (8)
- Accept that a different pace or way of processing does not mean someone needs your advice (9)

THE PORTRAIT OF A GIVER

ENNEAGRAM 2

"So this is the dance, it seems to me: to be the kind of host who honors the needs of the people who gather around his or her table, and to be the kind of guest who comes to the table to learn, not to demand."

—SHAUNA NIEQUIST

Introduction

Givers, or Enneagram 2s, are assumed to be the best at friendships due to their approachable disposition. In fact, in a poll I did of my Instagram followers, they ranked Givers as the Enneagram type they were most likely to befriend. Being wanted and desired is often the underlying motive of their behavior. But just because they are others-focused does not mean they easily fall into friendship. Though I know many Givers who have folks flocking to them like bees to honey, I also know many Givers who are extremely lonely—never feeling particularly known, even by those they are closest to.

Givers as a Friend when Healthy

When Givers are in a state of health, they are their compassionate self paired with self-awareness and self-sufficiency. Still others-focused, they balance their own well-being with taking care of others seamlessly. They lean into their natural optimism without fearing the darker, painful feelings they may have avoided in the past. Mixing their fiery boldness with gentle, tender presence, they no longer place their value as humans solely on their ability to love and help others. Increasingly crafty and passionate, they create for themselves as well as others.

Givers as a Friend when Coasting

When Givers are Coasting, not necessarily Healthy or unhealthy, they show the most stereotypical Enneagram 2 traits. Caring and expressive, they are unafraid of revealing the contents of their hearts to those they are close to. Similar to Dreamers, they tend to struggle with a push-and-pull in friendships, wanting others to be near them in a way where they are the ones in control of the pace of the friendship. Because of their natural bent toward sacrifice, others may find that Givers can also be a little moody and unexpected. Confused as to what they may have done wrong, others may not realize that Givers were expecting things in return from their selfless actions. Givers would never admit that they desire this, even though they deeply feel the need to receive from others in their heart of hearts.

Givers as a Friend when Stressed

When Givers are in a state of stress, they tend to express their frustration and agitation with how others have not shown up for them the way they have for others. When Givers lean into average to unhealthy traits of a Defender (Enneagram 8), others may feel like they are suddenly in a burning wildfire with their Giver, unaware of how the forest became inflamed to begin with. This is infuriating for Givers, because they believe how their brain works, how they serve and love others, should be common sense for everyone. They have a tendency to play the blame game, not seeing how they may have played a part in their burning frustration. Many Givers in this state have said they feel self-protecting, having to defend their seemingly selfless actions to those they are in tension with. Givers feel out of control when they are in this state, and they may try to regain control by becoming overbearing in their friendships and relationships.

Taking Care of a Giver

Tip #1: *Reach out first*

Givers are notoriously accessible individuals, maybe even to a fault. They are always there for you in your time of need and show up before you even know that you need them. Givers are a part of the Dutiful Stance of the Enneagram, which means that they feel a sense of moral obligation to those they love. They are typically not likely to cancel plans, and if they do, it is because of another person they feel responsible to take care of. Givers are often the first friend to reach out, and this can create a feeling of one-sidedness within their friendships. A challenge for those who want to care for the Givers in their life is to simply reach out first. Some of the other Enneagram types have great intentions of reaching out to the Givers in their life, but because they are used to the pattern of Givers reaching out to them, they can become apathetic or too reliant on a Giver's innate nature of reaching out. This exact cycle is what many Givers try to break, but they need your help! When Givers set up their personal boundaries and hear the crickets ringing from their phones, it shows them that the narrative they internalize about how they are only valued for what they do becomes a reality. Though this isn't often the case, realize that Givers need their friendships. It is a lifeblood for them. It is a Giver's responsibility to take care of themselves, but they also deserve to rely on those who are closest to them in their life. So, reach out first. Set reminders to reach out if you must.

Tip #2: *There's nothing wrong with being sensitive*

Givers are one of the most sensitive Enneagram types. I say this acknowledging it as a gift! Givers are empathetic and can place themselves in the shoes of those who are suffering with ease. This empathy drives them into action, making them the one to act in the wake of tragedy. This sensitivity bleeds into other areas of their life, including negative experiences. In friendships, Givers continually have their thumb on the pulse of the friendship and continually act to keep the pulse alive and well, even to their own detriment. To them, this gesture is meant to be endearing, but for some, it can feel smothering. The idea that their love as a Giver could feel smothering to someone else is soul-crushing. And when they are rejected because of their affection or display of love, it can cause them to spiral into depression. Though it is never your responsibility to own a Giver's personal experience, it is important to acknowledge as their friend, family member, or lover that their sensitivity to rejection is real. Givers are constantly absorbing your feelings toward them and feel lost without them when they are in an unhealthy state. To encourage a Giver who is struggling with rejection, put yourself in their shoes for a change. Try to understand their human experience the way they would for you. Better yet, take action. Make them their favorite meal. Gift them something small that made you think of them. Or even verbally acknowledge how you notice the power that the feeling of rejection holds over them. Feeling understood in their struggle with rejection will help create a safe place for Givers to feel more stable in their relationship with you.

Tip #3: *Remove hindrances to self-care*

Stereotypically, Givers are notoriously bad at self-care. Whether it be physical, mental, or spiritual, slowing down to care for themselves in the way they care for others proves to be a difficult task. However, many Givers online have expressed that being terrible at self-care doesn't always resonate with them. They have hobbies, they love to pamper themselves, and they have no problem watching a show they love or playing a video game they like simply for the joy of it. More accurately, Givers struggle with the hindrances that can often keep them from self-care. A huge weight to lift off your Giver's shoulders is the obstacle or obstacles that could keep them from self-care. That could be simply assisting with tasks like the dishes, laundry, getting gas, etc. Give them more than the bare minimum as well. Surprise them with a self-care basket or let them sleep in so you can bring breakfast in bed. Make space for them to invest in their passion or side project. Give them no other option but to love themselves.

Tip #4: *Surprise them*

In the same vein as Tip #3, surprising your Giver will greatly impact them and make them feel seen. Many Givers are uncomfortable with displays of affection or having to receive compliments, but there are other ways of surprising them with acts of love and appreciation beyond things that may make them cringe. Surprise them by listening to that album they love or learning more about their secret hobby. Surprise them by doing the chores they needed to do, plus having a self-care or romantic date night planned. For friends of Givers, think about what they would do for you: show up to your house with flowers, know you well enough to give you that perfect birthday gift, desire quality time like nobody's business. Gift them that quality time they're craving on a whim. Do your own research about cute friend or partner date ideas and set them up with your Giver. They will appreciate your effort more than you can imagine.

Tip #5: *Stay aware of the power dynamic*

Acknowledging a power dynamic in friendships and relationships with Givers may seem odd at first. Because Givers typically take a more modest stance, thinking that Givers dominate their relationships could sound foreign. But a power dynamic can look drastically different than the typical dominating force and the meek, small voice. Givers often unintentionally participate in a power dynamic by training others to need them because that is what they believe brings the most value to their relationships. This creates a cycle where Givers feel as though they are pouring out far more than they are receiving, causing burnout and strain in their relationships. Rather than remaining passively aware of this cycle, help Givers out by beginning to even things out in terms of how and what you give. This may be uncomfortable for the Giver at first, even if they are thankful for it. It may even trigger a worried reaction from them, but showing them how you are not going to let them be the only driving force in the relationship or friendship is healthiest for you both in the long run.

Becoming a Better Friend as a Giver

Tip #1: *Let go of shame*

The Givers that I have met in my life are naturals at friendship. They are always looking for ways to connect with others, and they seem to make themselves accessible with ease, perhaps too much ease. But this strength that Givers have often gets stereotyped or weaponized when it really should be celebrated. Givers can utilize this gift to help others become accessible, and it is time that Givers start viewing this part of themselves as a superpower. Of course, there are always boundaries that need to be set, and we'll even get to that later in the book, but Givers need to remember that their unique wiring and bent toward helping others is still their strength. Other people's struggle to be accessible is not your responsibility, and you are allowed to take up space and be accessible and be true to you in the process! There is a lot of pride to be held in answering the call to help when others simply would avoid the discomfort of it all.

Tip #2: *Access your true feelings*

Though Givers make themselves accessible through their time and actions, they often run into difficulties when they need to share their true feelings. A lot of people do not realize that Givers struggle with vulnerability, because they seem to be so open, but many emotional experiences that Givers share are reflections of what others are experiencing. Givers, rightfully so, sometimes believe that they are only valued in their friendships because of the way they care and hold others in their times of need. This belief inhibits them from being more accessible in their friendships, because many of them don't realize that their friends want their true feelings, not just their own feelings reflected back to them. Many Givers are not conscious that they do this, but because they are typically deep feelers, they can confuse the empathy they feel for others as their own emotional experience.

What Enneagram 2s experience as attending to the needs of others is far from being present with others. Paying attention through the lens of friendship requires more than attention to others—it requires attention to yourself. When I say attention to yourself, I don't mean self-consciousness. I mean what it looks like to take care of yourself in order to pay attention: to pay attention to take care. This could look like listening to your body in a conversation when it begins to feel activated or taking a step back before committing your help to someone in need. This can also mean pausing to examine your assumptions of other people's needs and why your instincts push you to act, rather than just be there for your friend.

Tip #3: *You are special regardless*
A frequent statement I hear from Givers is, "I don't know what I need." While I do believe this is true, I think many Givers actually do know how they want to be loved. Similarly to other types in the Heart Triad, they find themselves fantasizing over how they would go about loving or surprising themselves in both friendships and relationships. As a Giver, you probably have a list of dream dates, whether romantic or platonic, that you would love to embark on. You've probably dealt with a fair amount of disappointment when your partner or friend has not come up with the date or hangout ideas before you. There is a belief in many Givers that if another person does not love them in the exact way a Giver perceives they should, that the other person is doing it wrong. I am not referring to obvious relational red flags, but rather little things Givers do because it comes naturally to them. Some examples include what they bring to a host's house, what they give to their guests when they're at their own house, how should one go about giving flowers to someone else, sending love letters or packing sticky notes into a lunch, etc. For some other Enneagram types, thoughtfulness must be nurtured and discussed. That does not make them thoughtless, because there are a million other ways this friend or partner could be expressing love that you cannot see. Communicate what your love language is. Openly ask for what you desire from your friend or partner. They

want to love you and encourage you, but they may feel lost or scared of doing it wrong. Another challenge to Givers would be to take a full day and observe all the little ways your friend or partner loves you that you might overlook because it's not exactly how you pictured it. Maybe it's through acts of service or words of affirmation. . . . Find how they're attempting to love you and thank them for their effort! Take the time to learn the other's love language or secret wants as well, because your way of loving them may not be what they're desiring. And that's not your fault—helping and caring for others is all about communication and humility!

Tip #4: *Be pursued, too*

In a similar vein to a previous point, Givers can also put themselves in situations with finding friends that build a foundation of a power imbalance. Givers are called what they are because they are individuals who give of themselves, their resources, their interests, and more to experience friendship with others. They are the ultimate pursuers. When you are caught in a cycle of continuously pursuing others, you forget that you are also worthy of being pursued. Givers can forget that being pursued in friendship is just as important as pursuing because it creates a mutual connection as opposed to a one-sided connection. In a 2023 poll I did on Instagram about Enneagram types and burnout, almost every Giver expressed experiencing fatigue from how aggressively intentional they are in their relationships as outlined above. So, as I invite your friends and loved ones to reach out to you first, take time to focus less on your availability. Turn your phone to "Do Not Disturb" and have a staycation with just yourself. Whether you need to rot on the couch or hike a 14er, find what you need to do to revitalize your soul. Let yourself feel when you worry about not being pursued. In order to retrain the friends in your life to not rely on you for making plans, you will have to break the cycle.

. . . .

Tip #5: *You can handle rejection*

Givers have a unique relationship with disappointment. It is said that within the Enneagram personality typing system, Givers, Investigators, and Defenders have the hardest time dealing with rejection. Specifically for Givers, who are in the Heart Triad, rejection is a viscerally emotional experience. As mentioned previously, disappointment can be a major distraction for Givers in relationships. Often, it is the built-up disappointment of a partner or friend not fully seeing and knowing them in the way they would've hoped. Every Enneagram type has a feeling that they believe they cannot survive experiencing. For Givers, this feeling is rejection, but they can handle it. Givers often lose sight of their strengths and their value apart from how they serve others. You can survive rejection, not just because you are strong, but because you are more than your relationships.

Approaching Conflict with a Giver

You may experience conflict with a Giver because . . .

- If you are an Improver, they seem to enable others and neglect themselves
- If you are a fellow Giver, it may feel like a competition of who is the most helpful and irreplaceable
- If you are a Doer, their desire to help can feel invasive or deceitful
- If you are a Seeker, they seem to care more about how they can help over how you feel
- If you are an Investigator, they seem to not respect your need for space
- If you are an Advocate, their loyalty may come across as disingenuous
- If you are an Explorer, they don't seem to understand your boundaries
- If you are a Defender, they seem to be too sensitive
- If you are a Peacemaker, they seem to overreact and over-expect

As a Giver, you may experience conflict . . .
- With an Improver, because they seem to put criticism before compassion
- With a fellow Giver, because you feel like there isn't enough room for the both of you
- With a Doer, because they seem to avoid emotional intimacy
- With a Seeker, because their focus on their personal experience feels selfish
- With an Investigator, because you seem to have to prove you are worthy of their energy
- With an Advocate, because they seem to pull away from the relationship because of their worries
- With an Explorer, because they seem to not care as deeply as you about things
- With a Defender, because they seem to not care about how their actions affect others
- With a Peacemaker, because you feel like you're the only one making an effort

We can't control the behavior of others, BUT here is what you can do . . .
- Learn detachment from the values of others; it might help you discover your own (1)
- Have empathy for the pressure you both feel in your relationships; there is room for both of you (2)
- Remember that being emotionally intimate is not as easy for others as it may be for you (3)
- Understand that personal expression does not mean you are selfish (4)
- Learn to respect their internal processing (5)

- Remember that sometimes others need space to bond (6)
- Understand that people cope differently; both ways can be Healthy or unhealthy! (7)
- Realize that another's strength doesn't minimize yours (8)
- Resign from your role as caretaker and learn to just be (9)

THE PORTRAIT OF A DOER

ENNEAGRAM 3

Introduction

Type 3s, or Doers, are at the center of the Heart Triad of the Enneagram. Joined by Givers and Seekers, Doers are also motivated by their emotions, though they and others may not see this at first. Because Doers are the anchor point for the Heart Triad, they struggle more than the other types in this Triad with staying connected to their true emotions. Typically charming, motivated, and goal-oriented, Doers are often the visionaries and leaders in our environment. They typically have a wide network of connections and want to be seen as hardworking individuals. Their image-consciousness usually makes them rather trendy folks, determined to find the best restaurants, the best brands, etc. Doers are driven by the desire to be valuable, impactful, and admired. This is because they fear being worthless or being seen as worthless by others. To cope with this fear, they create a pathway toward numbing their real feelings and needs for the purpose of their image, success, and appearance. While this may sound superficial, Doers' sacrificing of their emotions goes far deeper than other Enneagram types realize. Their image or appearance not only has to do with physical attributes, but also with how others view them in general. Doers may have experienced a lack of unconditional presence or attention from a caregiver growing up, or perhaps they were put under a lot of pressure at an early age to earn the approval of a caregiver or authority figure. A Doer's drive for attention and affirmation comes from a sense of acceptance and unconditional love being based on the approval of their actions. This is why so many Doers find themselves tailoring an image that is suitable to whoever they are within the moment, taking pride in their adaptability without seeing its shadow side.

Doers as a Friend when Healthy

In a Healthy state, Doers still find themselves motivated by a need to be valuable, but it shows up differently in their behavior. Their drive to be hardworking and "the best" extends to a desire to also be a team player who helps others also be encouraged and successful. As they heal their childhood wounds, they establish a balance between moving forward and pausing for reflection. Continuing to grow, they become increasingly less afraid of simply "being," able to embrace themselves and others regardless of what gain or connection could be had. Far more emotionally vulnerable, Doers are less prone to avoiding or numbing how they feel in favor of allowing themselves to be truly seen by someone they love, understanding the value of loyalty and community, beginning to cultivate roots with a group they care about and relate with, and allowing themselves to be exposed in favor of being known and loved. Celebratory and empowering, Doers begin to match others' pace as opposed to forcing others to match theirs. Showing up unashamed as their authentic self and learning to embrace failure, they take their emotional experiences and use them for the benefit of the common good.

Doers as a Friend when Coasting

When Doers are Coasting, neither in a state of health or a state of stress, their typical Doer traits are paired with an open suspicion and competitiveness regarding their friendships and relationships. Emotional vulnerability in this state tends to look like venting or openly expressing their worries or dissatisfaction. Though Doers are incredibly charismatic and positive individuals, as friends, they may be more prone to displaying a negative attitude or complaining in secret about their priorities and their obligations. This is when Doers get caught up in the competition of life, working to be the best employee, best leader, best friend, spouse, child, coworker, you name it! While they know there is abundance in life for all, they engage and enable their scarcity mindset to move themselves into action.

Doers as a Friend when Stressed

In Stress, Doer qualities are met with a version of themselves they are always presenting to others. This version may feel staged, robotic, or inauthentic to those they care about the most, but Doers are numb to what is going on inside and around them, solely focused on what they are producing and how they are appearing to others. This leads to Doers sticking to plans or pursuing goals out of complete obligation, not genuine interest, almost like being trapped on an escalator, unsure of what floor to finally step off on. Refusing to seek or accept help from others during this time, many Doers keep up their facade as "the best" from the outside looking in, while completely withdrawing and shutting down when alone. Leaning into the average to unhealthy aspects of Peacemakers, Doers actively engage in numbing their feelings by vegging and zoning out. This causes feelings of purposelessness and loneliness in Doers, which may cause them to spiral into feelings of depression. The hardest part of this state of being for Doers is that many of them may believe that since they are appearing successful to others, it doesn't matter who they are at home or what they are feeling. Playing the part and maintaining the smoke and mirrors becomes where they place most of their energy as they drift further and further from their true, authentic self.

Taking Care of a Doer

Tip #1: *Set clear expectations*

As many of us have probably experienced, Doers are individuals who have places to go, meetings to attend, and people to see. They are typically very busy people who have cast their net wide in terms of friendships and obligations to others. This is why setting clear expectations with them will go a long way in the long run when pursuing any type of long-term interpersonal relationship with a Doer. Because Doers are goal-oriented people, they may tend to view your relationship or friendship through this lens. This doesn't necessarily mean they will engage with you superficially, but it does mean they like to know where you stand within the relationship pretty early on. I truly believe that Doers want to show up in a genuine way for their people, which can lead them to over-promise things to those they love. Though it is not your responsibility to keep them from over-promising, setting clear expectations and boundaries up front from the beginning will keep Doers from reading between the lines.

Tip #2: *Help them embrace failure*

I remember being taken aback by an Instagram post a couple of years ago regarding Doers. A woman had commented on someone's post talking about her daughter, whom she was assuming to be a Doer because of her behavior and fears. She said one of the main things she has noticed in her daughter is her crippling fear of not only failure but failing in front of others. Doers are deeply affected by the emotional experience of embarrassment. When this woman noticed this in her daughter, she sprang into action. She began making every Saturday "Fail Saturday." She would take her daughter to new activities, experiences, or hobbies she was too nervous to try for fear of failure, and they would embark on the journey together. I specifically remember her saying something along the lines of, "I wanted her to see that failure often leads to progress. And that a life avoiding failure is a life stuck in a box." This Instagram comment and discussion has stuck with me for years, and I hope it encourages both Doers and friends and loved ones of Doers. Come alongside them as they grow their emotional tolerance in the face of failure or embarrassment. Show them they are more than the self-consciousness they feel.

Tip #3: *Value their true feelings*

Because Doers are used to numbing their emotions or even copying the emotional presentation of others under stress, it can be a visceral experience for a partner or close friend of a Doer when they truly share what is on their heart. Because Doers are preoccupied with how they appear to others, the act of sharing their feelings in a pure way takes a lot of effort, perhaps the most effort out of all the Enneagram types. Pay attention to what Doers do in moments of vulnerability and pure expression, because this can help inform you about their behavioral patterns in the future. Doers have a hard time staying grounded in their own values as opposed to the values they believe they should have. When you pay attention to the vulnerability of a Doer, it will allow you to speak into their life when they need to be reminded of who they are and what they truly want.

Tip #4: *Create an environment for "just being"*

In almost every Enneagram book I've read or skimmed, there is a portion of the Doer chapter that talks about "being" versus "doing." *Take Care of Your Type*, my first book, even makes mention of this for Doers. It is talked about for a reason, but it can also be frustrating for Doers to hear repeatedly, especially if they primarily are the ones taking initiative in their relationships or in their obligations. For Doers to just "be," it is also necessary for someone to fulfill the leadership roles they typically fill. If you want your Doer to relax and recover, give them the space and create an environment where they feel as though they can let their hair down. Maybe your Doer's guilty pleasure is video games, but they never allow themselves to play for fear of looking lazy. Or perhaps they want to pick up their hobby of baking again, but they are too afraid of looking incompetent in front of the person they love. Approach these scenarios with empathy and willingness to give your Doer space as they explore being themselves beyond what they produce.

Tip #5: *Be patient in waiting for the mask to fall*

Writing the Doer chapter is difficult for me because Doers are one of the Enneagram types I personally have a hard time relating to. Some of the most hurtful words and deeds that have been said and done to me have been done by unhealthy Doers, and this causes me to have my guard up typically when I interact with a Doer, regardless of age or gender. However, through these experiences, I have also had the privilege of witnessing Doers as their mask of being impactful falls to the floor—when their real laugh echoes through a hallway, when they discuss a painful childhood memory, when they get excited about a song they care about. When Doers are in a Healthy state, they are willing and communicate with you honestly. In fact, they prefer to lay down the facades and be vulnerable. As a friend, it is important to remember that this may take time for your Doer to feel comfortable with, especially if they are in a Coasting or Stressed state. But I promise that when the mask falls, and it will, it will be worth your while!

Becoming a Better Friend as a Doer

Tip #1: *Don't rely on energy alone*

Though the typical stereotype for Doers is that they are workaholics, many of them do struggle with workaholic tendencies in unhealthy seasons of their lives. It can be easy for Doers to mistake their ability to network with others as their way of finding friendships. It's not impossible to find friends while networking, but there are significant differences in getting to know someone for their abilities versus getting to know someone for who they are. Doers ideally like to be around people who make them feel like an elevated version of themselves. One could argue that they enjoy the status, but I think it has more to do with enjoying the security of other people perceiving them as worthy. While pursuing connections that make them feel elevated, they can forget that feeling elevated is not the same as feeling seen. As a Doer, it is important to remember that some of the most cherished people in your life may be the ones that seemingly slow you down, or the ones who may have a different exterior status than you. They may value work less and play more. Do not translate someone's ability to keep your pace as their worthiness of your intention.

Tip #2: *Emotional presence matters*

An irreplaceable bond grows quickly between people you can count on seeing in the same place, at the same time, every week. I was in a little group like this for many years where the language became nicknames and inside jokes, belly laughing deeply together at the most ridiculous things, and sharing similar beliefs and passions. Yet no matter how closely I laughed with this group, or how much I had memorized the language of its camaraderie, I always felt on the outside of the shared connection. It made no sense to me.

I tried so hard to connect and fit in. I wanted to enjoy what was being enjoyed by the group, and it felt like there was a roadblock to my getting there.

"I feel like we're finally seeing you."
When this was said to me, it was after years of working with the same group of people. I was stunned to hear this sentence, because it put into words how I had been feeling internally for many years. I started digging into a few factors that I think sparked a deeper connection than before. I realized that with gradual comfort and consistency, I had begun to unmask my true self. I was focused less on proving I belonged. I was less distracted with how I was coming across and more focused on just being with this group of people. You can be in the right place at the right time with the right people and still be inaccessible regarding friendship, simply because of self-consciousness. My advice to Doers who may also be struggling with this relational pattern is to feel a sense of urgency surrounding vulnerability. Suspend your belief into trusting that others truly care for and want to know the real you. Your real thoughts, feelings, and opinions. Your real Spotify Wrapped. Feel an urgency to be who you are authentically in all situations; you may be surprised how much deeper your current connections become because of it.

Tip #3: *The best is not easy*

Many Doers do not relate to the stereotypical view of Doers, such as Doers being CEOs or intense corporate leaders of any kind. The truth is that although Doers desire to be the best, their energy can be allocated in many different avenues besides their careers. Many Doers tend to direct their interest in being the best toward their relationships, wanting the best friendship, the best partner, and wanting to be the best friend, partner, parent, etc. for someone else. Theoretically, this is good for relationships, but it can quickly become an obstacle when a Doer is in an unhealthy state of being. The desire to be the best can cause Doers to act superficially in their friendships, wanting to look and feel the best even if that is not the truth. The truth that Doers need to realize is that the best is not easy. Fighting for the best relationship or friendship takes work and dedication beyond maintaining physical evidence of connection. Redefining what a best relationship looks like takes realizing that vulnerability and consistency will take you far. Your friendship or relationship may tick off all the boxes of things it is supposed to be, but is it honest? Is it safe? Is it authentic? Practice showing up authentically as yourself in your relationships regardless of how it feels or looks or falls into your categories of "best." One day, you will look up and see how much working toward "real" will bring you the "best."

Tip #4: *Don't wait for the breakdown*

Though I do not think Rory Gilmore, one of the main characters from the TV show *Gilmore Girls,* was a Doer, I think she is an amazing example of a character who marked her life and identity by achievements. She had to be the daughter Richard and Emily never had, while being the daughter Lorelai hoped to be. We see Rory throughout the later seasons unable to keep up appearances. She struggles to receive feedback from others and do what is morally right when it comes to her relationships. She deceives herself into thinking she isn't falling apart or having a crisis, because she was never given permission to do so. The moment her humanity showed in her adolescence, it was shamed away with, "But think about your future." I see this pattern in a myriad of ways with Doers, because it is often only once they completely break down that they give themselves permission to rest, to feel, to recover—you name it! My challenge for Doers is to take a step toward rest and healing and feeling now. Do not keep waiting for the breakdown. It seems obvious that stepping away from the cliff's edge will prevent the fall, but it's hard to know overexercising, overworking, over-fill-in-the-blank is a cliff until it's too late. Your loved ones are happy to catch you when you fall. Surprise them with your willingness to slow down every once in a while. It is to the benefit of your long-term health!

Tip #5: *The distraction of obligation*

Doers enjoy having many close relationships in their lives. Many of them love meeting new people and usually have a relatively booked social calendar. As much as this can bring a Doer joy, an obstacle to deepening relationships in their social calendar is the feeling of obligation toward the socializing they are doing. They may love to meet others for dinner, or they used to love the book club they signed up for months ago; since it's important for Doers to keep up appearances, this can cause them to stay in groups or clubs they feel an obligation to as opposed to feeling a sense of enjoyment for being in. If you are a Doer and find yourself disconnected and unsatisfied in your relationships, it may be time to reevaluate your social calendar from a lens of enjoyment as opposed to obligation. Perhaps having a full calendar does not equal having a full heart. Say no more to unnecessary obligations that keep up appearances and say yes to more nurturing of your core friendships and relationships.

Approaching Conflict with a Doer

You may experience conflict with a Doer because . . .
- If you are an Improver, they seem to care more about their image as opposed to their integrity
- If you are a Giver, they seem to be emotionally unavailable
- If you are a fellow Doer, you're both trying to be the best
- If you are a Seeker, their ambition seems inauthentic
- If you are an Investigator, they seem to ignore practicality and rationality
- If you are an Advocate, they seem untrustworthy
- If you are an Explorer, they seem to only care about praise and validation
- If you are a Defender, you feel like you see right through their BS
- If you are a Peacemaker, their focus on continual growth is stressful

As a Doer, you may experience conflict . . .
- With an Improver, because it seems like you can't do anything right with them
- With a Giver, because their desire to help you feels invasive
- With a fellow Doer, because you simultaneously bring out the best and worst in each other
- With a Seeker, because it feels like they get in their own way

- With an Investigator, because their approach to life feels too slow
- With an Advocate, because they seem to be needy and close-minded
- With an Explorer, because they seem like they don't care about anything that they are doing
- With a Defender, because desiring leadership doesn't mean you have to be cruel
- With a Peacemaker, because they seem to not do anything about the issues they're having in their life

We can't control the behavior of others, BUT here is what you, as a Doer, can do . . .

- Consider that accuracy and efficiency can coexist (1)
- Remember that someone wanting to connect with you or offer help does not mean you are incapable (2)
- Have empathy for the shared experience of not feeling like enough; support each other! (3)
- Learn that self-reflection can lead to more progress (4)
- Understand that taking a step back to observe can benefit you in the long run (5)
- Remember that it is not only OK, but important to be interrupted with concerns for safety and the common good (6)
- Accept that feeling purpose in life isn't one-size-fits-all (7)
- Learn from the ability to speak directly and unapologetically when done healthily (8)
- Remember that restfulness and growth inherently go together (9)

ENNEAGRAM 4

Introduction

Seekers, whether extroverted or introverted, value real connections with others. I don't think every Seeker is writing sonnets for their loved ones with their instrument of choice, but I do think that Seekers feel a lot regarding the people they care about. So much so that it overflows in either creative expression or deep empathy. Seekers as individuals are a part of the Heart Triad, making them one of the Enneagram types that struggles with the over- or under-expression of their emotions. Though there are exceptions for every personality type, I do think most Seekers struggle with the overexpression of their emotions because of how physically they feel them. A superpower of Seekers in their relationships is their ability to sit with their friends no matter what life is throwing at them. Seekers are the first ones to sing and dance and twirl and celebrate with you in light of a joyous occasion, and they are the first to cry and hold hands with you when you are facing a tumultuous season.

Once Seekers realize that they can come to their own rescue, life will suddenly look much brighter than before. Because it was never about someone else saving them from themselves–it was about accepting themselves as who they are despite their feelings, despite their longing. The reason this is such a pivotal point in the Seeker's story is because they believe that they can be a hero. They are not a villain or side character or NPC. They are the main event— their life is the main event. Accepting their suffering can turn all the parts they're ashamed of into self-acceptance. They were never lacking anything, they were never in need of rescue. . . . They were simply in need of unconditional love.

Seekers as a Friend when Healthy

When Seekers are Healthy, they can show up for their friendships consistently. They become very insightful, objectively analyzing issues others are facing in tandem with their empathy. As opposed to constantly needing novelty and nostalgia as a fuel for connection, they embrace the mundane joys of being in community with others–the basic check-in texts, the routine hangouts. There are no worries about how the Seeker feels in the absence of emotional conversation, because they are secure in themselves and in you. They are grounded in their approach to helping and listening, realizing that others feel just as deeply as they do, even if it is not expressed in the same way. Finding this level of balance and security, a Seeker's empathy shines brightly into the lives of those they love.

Seekers as a Friend when Coasting

When Seekers are Coasting, not in survival mode but not necessarily thriving, they find themselves battling the reconciliation of how they feel to how others may feel. Though they never lose their empathy, it tends to be more focused on their own personal experiences in life and in relationships, disbelieving that others feel to the same degree or understand what they may be going through. Because of this, they can become more vocally critical about themselves and about others. Like Improvers, Seekers in this mode of being will see their own flaws and the flaws of others before the positives. They become picky and impatient, making sure that how they are presenting themselves and what relationships they are involved in are perfectly aligned with their authentic selves.

Seekers as a Friend when Stressed

When Seekers are in survival mode, it will affect their friendships in a myriad of ways. They will still internally experience the same core desires and fears as a typical Seeker, but their behavior may start to look like that of an unhealthy Giver, an Enneagram 2. Many Seekers struggle with a push-and-pull cycle, and this is particularly evident when a Seeker is in survival mode or an unhealthy state of being. They will cling to their loved ones for dear life, only to withhold their affection from them to test the other's commitment to the relationship. They may become the first one to show up and the last one to leave, continually doing favors for others in hopes that they recognize the value they bring to their relationships. Seekers struggle with comparison, and this will show itself through possessiveness and jealousy, causing those in friendships with Seekers to feel like they are walking on eggshells. Though toxic behavior is never excused, it can be explained. When Seekers are in this state of survival mode, their self-worth plummets to an all-time low. Seekers fight with a tension in their hearts—always feeling like something is inherently wrong with them. When Seekers are unhealthy, they search for their wholeness in the context of their relationships. "Maybe I am the missing piece to someone else's puzzle, or maybe someone else is the missing piece to mine." When this rescue of sorts does not go as planned, Seekers see that the narrative they internalized is in fact the truth: that there will be no feeling of completion for them, and that they are destined to be lacking forever.

Seekers can be incredible friends with a capacity for deep joy and deep sorrow.

Taking Care of a Seeker

Tip #1: *Express yourself with them*
What many people do not understand about Seekers is how much their internal emotions affect them. It is a visceral experience, one that feels like their brain is rattling and their heart is physically aching. Many Seekers suffer from chronic overexpression because of this. Whether it be through an art form, physical movement, or conversations—it sometimes feels like they won't survive the storm inside them unless they get it out. A hard pill for Seekers to swallow is how sometimes they need to feel their feelings. This may be a shocking truth for

a Seeker to hear, since they may feel like they already feel their feelings so well. But they express their feelings, as opposed to feeling them. Seekers may believe that not expressing their emotions is suppression, but that is a very black-and-white way to think. Feeling your feelings, letting them live in your body, letting them take up space while choosing to believe that the feeling will end soon, is not emotional suppression. It's emotional intelligence, emotional discernment.

Even if receiving another's full self and full emotions is difficult for a Seeker at first, that truly is what they desire from other people in moments of cele-bration and weakness. They want to process and dissect who others are and how they work. They want to know others' opposing ways of processing. They adjust to how others process because they want them to cry and laugh and feel as much as they do in whatever way that looks like for everyone as a unique indi-vidual. As much as Seekers long to be understood, they also long to understand others. Many Seekers find themselves interested in subjects like psychology for this reason. To psychoanalyze is to show love for a Seeker; when done healthily, this can be a superpower within a relationship. So, if you know a Seeker, express your not-so-nuanced opinions. Rant about the thing that's been keeping you up at night. Cry happy tears over something you saw on your commute home. It's a Seeker's dream to be let into your expression. It makes them feel accepted, loved, and trusted.

Tip #2: *Divert their attention from flaws*
Similarly to Improvers, Seekers have a very idealistic view of the world. Influenced by movies, books, or whatever media they consume, their ideas sur-rounding themselves and relationships with other people are often compared to their dreamlike view of the world. Because of this, friends of Seekers may view them as individuals who live in a fantasized version of reality. This fantasiz-ing of relationships causes Seekers to pendulum-swing back and forth between

extreme optimism and extreme disappointment. They bask in their rose-colored filter of their relationship until comparison breaks through like a bucket of black paint. Once comparison has splattered over their idealism, it is very difficult for Seekers to bounce back from their disappointment. Their assumptions about relationships will go from, "Everything will always be wonderful and exactly how I pictured it," to "Everything will be a nightmare and I will never experience what I've dreamt of for so long." Seekers may have a blind spot as to how this pendulum swing affects those in their life. If you happen to be on this roller coaster with a Seeker, my advice to you wouldn't be to buckle up and take it, but it also isn't to ditch the ride completely. There is a level of validity to a Seeker's fear, so the goal isn't to change how they are wired, but to disengage from the behaviors that harm both you and them.

When Seekers are in a healthier headspace, they are some of the best people to go and find hope in the darkness. If they have gone deep and learned how to come up stronger, they are who you want in your corner when you need to come up for air in the thick of hurt. If you can, lean into this quality of a Seeker and reflect it back to them. Remind them that they are more than the flaws they are focusing on, that they have overcome so much, despite things not being exactly what they had hoped. Connect a few dots for them as to how life is still bright and alive around them; I guarantee they will poetically find their way back to hope if they have your hand to hold.

Tip #3: *Go deep*

2016 - my fave book

A misconception about Seekers is that because they seem to express themselves so deeply, there is nothing left for someone else to do except nod, agree, listen, etc. Seekers may even come across as intimidating with how much awareness they seem to have about their human experience. The reality is, Seekers tend to overanalyze and intellectualize their emotions, and they may even have gotten to the bottom of something without you. But Seekers love to know what you think about their exploration of the depths. Seekers tend to feel immense amounts of shame about their mission of self-discovery and awareness. Sometimes it is the thing that holds them back from their breakthroughs; other times it has been dismissed as unwanted or unnecessary by others. There is a bittersweetness to a Seeker's exploration of the depths—as much as they can enjoy it, it is also their haunting ghost.

A couple of months ago, my dear friend and I were casually discussing the topic of mental health. On this specific occasion, she asked me to go into detail about my experience living with OCD. Often when this has happened to me in the past, I worry about oversharing or being too real. Regardless, I answered every one of her questions with sincerity and honesty. I tried to avoid my tendency to overshare, but I still acted as myself in our conversation. After I shared, my friend gave such a kindhearted, genuine reaction to the depth

I had shared. She had been soaking up every word and had even deeper points to make, along with follow-up questions. It made me feel cared for and understood in that moment. Not because she suddenly understood OCD and all its complexities, but because she took the time to understand how OCD is a part of my human experience. She went there with me. My friend was able to sit in my depths while remaining curious about where the light shines through it. And that, my friends, is why everyone (especially Seekers) needs someone to give them hope and a hand to hold. They need a lantern in the darkness, reminding them that things aren't as scary as they feel. Going deep is not just how you show you care, but how you can show them that they can find the light with you.

Tip #4: *Romanticize the mundane*
"Enjoy it," Noah, my husband, said to me as he did a goofy dance down our hallway. To motivate myself to write, I made s'mores and poured tea and turned on a "Dark Academia & Royal Core" playlist on Spotify to convince me that I'm not writing my book in our crowded guest/storage room because our basement flooded. On the contrary! I am in the coziest, most magnificent of libraries, focused, calm, and brilliant.

A Seeker's desire to be so deeply connected to the magic of life is often weaponized against them, because a Seeker does not just cower in the darkness, they soak up the light. They want others to soak it up with them. The joy of their favorite scene in a movie. The song that they can't listen to without crying. It is all significant to them because they believe the small things ought to be significant. When this behavior is not used to over-spiritualize or stir the pot, it is a great service to others who may have a hard time seeing their lives through the color and scent of roses.

Rather than criticizing and judging a Seeker for living in a fantasy world, I want to challenge you to step into their daydreams with them. These daydreams can enforce longing, but they can also heal a lot of pain. Celebrate the mundane moments with them; spice up the ordinary before they do. The fantasy they have created can teach you a lot about who they are and what they are going through. It is a vulnerable picture of their heart—if they are letting you into their romantic worldview, you are precious and treasured by them.

Tip #5: *Show grace in the face of their sensitivity*

My all-time favorite movie is *You've Got Mail*. Tough and tender businessman Joe Fox meets soft and twirly bookshop keeper Kathleen Kelly; the tropes today do not compare to the magical ride this movie takes me on every time I watch it. As I've grown older, I've seen my character reflected a lot in the character of Kathleen: her depth, her dreamy view of the world, and her utter denial to the demands of reality. I relate to her thought process: this is my mom's store, and she passed it on to me—why would the universe take them both away? For Kathleen, and for many Seekers, the world can be too harsh to bear sometimes.

One of my favorite scenes from the film is when Joe comes to make amends with Kathleen after his company puts her bookstore out of business. He comes pursuing friendship, even though we as the viewer know he is hopelessly in love with her. He brings her a bouquet of daises, her favorite flower, and they sit across from each other in the living room as Kathleen, sick with the flu, gives this speech . . .

JOE: It wasn't…personal.

KATHLEEN: What is that supposed to mean? I am so sick of that. All that means is that it wasn't personal to you. But it was personal to me. It's "personal" to a lot of people. And what's so wrong with being personal anyway?

JOE: Uh, nothing.

KATHLEEN: Whatever else anything is, it ought to begin by being personal.

Here, we are observing Kathleen in a moment of radical honesty. You can tell in Joe's eyes that he knew he was now upon sacred ground; he had witnessed a piece of her heart and sensitivity firsthand. And he holds it.

What many friends and partners of Seekers fail to realize is that Seekers simply want you to hold their sensitivity with grace. A Seeker is in touch with their emotions, but they also simultaneously feel guilty for being in tune with them. Being affected by life and the cruelness of it or the magic of it is often labeled as cringe-y or too much. Seekers contain this tension within themselves, despite finding relief in expressing it. When a Seeker expresses their sensitivity with you, the best response you can have is the one that is furthest from being shame-inducing. Talk about daisies. Hold their hand. Don't be afraid to lean into the sensitivity with them. The epiphanies they have in this process are unparalleled. And it is this sensitivity that motivates individuals to deliver babies, care for the elderly, and paint masterpieces.

Becoming a Better Friend as a Seeker

Tip #1: *Expression isn't always vulnerable*

If you are a Seeker, you are well-acquainted with how feelings settle in your bones. No matter how big or small the thought, action, or event, the raging sea that rises inside you often feels as though it will overpower your entire being. Noah recently told me that when he sees me cry or become overcome with emotion about something, it is helpful for him because I'm displaying what he is feeling versus showing. This got my wheels turning, because though I cannot measure how much feelings ache within him, it had me wondering about this idea of Seekers being "deeper" than the other types. Their ability to feel and feel deeply is a Seeker's catalyst to connection. But I'm beginning to wonder if this infantilization of emotions might lead to inaccessibility. What if there is a facade of vulnerability in the art of expression?

To express means to put thoughts into words or to reveal. Seekers have become notorious for expressing their emotions, but what if emotions are not actually what we are expressing? There is a term in psychology called "intellectualization of feelings." Intellectualization is defined as a defense mechanism people use to avoid confronting difficult emotions such as sadness, anger, shame, etc. Through the art of expressing what is inside, many Seekers have lost connection to how they feel about what they are expressing. Seekers go on self-loathing rants, soapboxes of passion—they claim to display their tears without fear, craving intensity more than most. But I believe Seekers rely on the thrill of intensity or expression to avoid confronting their shame head-on.

Just like every other number on the Enneagram, Seekers have this facade of vulnerability, expressing only what they want to express, using expression as a way to avoid the pain emotions bring up in their body. This affects a Seeker's friendships, because it can make getting to know the real them almost impossible for those they love. Seekers can get so busy with expressing that they leave little to no room for others to respond. To help. To join them.

Tip #2: *Flaws do not define you or others*

Enneagram 4s tend to over-identify with their suffering. It's like a scab they can't help but pick, whether that is comparing, expressing, or suppressing it. They seem to hold a secret belief that suffering will gain them access to belonging. For some 4s, that can look like oversharing their suffering or playing the victim more frequently than they would admit. And for other 4s, it looks like being overly resilient—internalizing every ounce of hardship. Seekers, you are more than your suffering. You are more than your emotions. You are more to your friends than both of those things. You do not have to suffer through your friendships to find acceptance.

Though there is a sense of long-suffering when it comes to friendships, friendships need not be something that you suffer through. I've learned this the hard way through experiencing friendships that I thought I had to endure for the sake of enduring. Due to their tendency to romanticize, Seekers may struggle with idealizing difficult relationships as a way to cope with their pain.

When Seekers are in the trenches of their relationships, the overidentification with their suffering can also lead to the hyperfixation on flaws. This keeps Seekers from being present in their relationships. Who am I without the suffering I experience from simply being me? Who am I without the suffering inflicted upon me by someone else? Who am I without the narrative I have created that lives constantly within my internal world? These are all questions you as a Seeker must face to experience comfort in your relationships. Another path Seekers can go down is the one of isolation. "Nothing will ever be what I imagined, so I might as well go it alone." I personally have fallen into the trap of this way of thinking, desiring to remain single not because I genuinely wanted that, but because of the demands a real, loving, healthy relationship might bring to my life. Relationships take us out of ourselves and into the messy, gorgeous chaos of love and community. Focusing on flaws and/or unnecessarily suffering for your relationships is a roundabout way of avoiding steps of bravery. The healing you desire comes from the eyes no longer focusing on the wrinkles and imperfections; lift your head from the study of whys, hows, and what ifs. Tap into your deep desire to see and sense the beauty in the world and find it outside of the universe in your mind. Find it in the freckles on your best friend's cheeks and the belly laugh of your partner of three years. Dig into your fear of the present by forcing yourself to be present as opposed to analyzing the present.

Tip #3: *Be intentional regardless of perceived depth*

From a young age, I struggled with small talk and inside jokes. I was always scanning the way I conducted myself in social interactions to figure out if I was teasing well enough or speaking shallow enough. Once the conversation crossed a barrier from "hello" and "what weather we're having today," I found it much easier to relax and express myself in interactions with others. One of the admittedly toxic ways I dealt with my social anxiety was taking out my imaginary ruler and measuring the depth in others throughout my interactions. Did they talk about their dreams as passionately as I did? Were they in tune with their emotions?

When interacting with fellow Seekers online, I see this as a common thread among us. One of the hardest parts about remaining intentional with our relationships is when we feel like our depth is not being received, or we are unimpressed with the depth of another. This can foster a superiority complex for a Seeker despite their low self-esteem. In fact, this measurement of depth can be one of the only positive things Seekers feel about themselves when they are in states of stress or unhealth. I don't want to communicate here that putting boundaries in place to keep yourself safe and mentally healthy is a bad thing. In fact, being open and available to every human being is unsustainable and exhausting. But for many Seekers, their trial period of depth before enforcing a boundary can be rather short. In fact, I would say this "boundary" looks more like a bridge across a moat. There is a troll enforcing the laws of depth for all of those who wish to enter. Those who do not pass have the bridge cranked out from under them, leaving the castle walls locked and overgrown.

Put away the ruler of depth and replace it with intentional compassion. Utilize your skills of self-reflection to understand why a "lack of depth" frightens or triggers you. Could it be that others do not assign their inherent worth to their ability to be insightful? Often, our treatment of others is a reflection of our own hearts—in this case, what is in yours? In the past, you may have had to prove that you are valuable and worthy of attention through your ability to feel and be profound, but these are narratives that belong in the past. It is time to take up a new understanding of yourself and others. You deserve intentionality with every silly, unimportant comment as much as the next person. And others deserve your attention regardless of whether they are on "your level."

Tip #4: *Community matters*

As someone who is ADHD, I have a hard time developing habits, to say the least. I can dream up who I look like when I have good habits. I can do all the planning, purchasing, and researching, but executing on a consistent basis can feel like going against my nature. Though a Seeker has the ability to embrace the beauty of a good habit, the dedication becomes difficult when the novelty wears off. This can happen to Seekers in their relationships, too; the freshness or stimulation from a connection or community can directly impact a Seeker's willingness to stay invested. Because what is the point of hanging out if you don't go deep? What is the point of gathering if all you do is remain on the surface of conversation?

If there's anything Monday night dinner has taught me, it's that consistency pays off more than novelty ever will. Conversations do not always have to go deep for them to be meaningful. There does not have to be a profound realization or breakthrough in friendships for them to last. It is often the menial, everyday moments that build a pillar of connection. So don't wait for the movie moment. Don't try to create the movie moment, either. Simply exist on the couch. Visit your friend, even if silence is all that remains between you. Make it a habit to be in the community, and one day you'll look around and realize you're living the magical moments you've always dreamt of!

Tip #5: *Let go of longing*

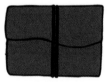

Throughout this chapter, we're seeing the impacts of longing on a Seeker's life. Coping with reality can look like daydreaming, longing, and romanticization for most Seekers, fantasizing about big, cinematic, relational moments that may never happen. Amid conflict as a Seeker, there may be a tendency to dream up a scenario in which they receive the perfect apology. Or they might have the ideal make-up conversation where everything goes exactly to plan and is expressed how it needed to be expressed. This can stir up feelings of longing within Seekers in situations where grace needs to be given. There are times when amazing friends will disappoint and won't go about expressing their feelings in the way Seekers wanted them to. I think there is a big difference in letting friends go because you know that's the right thing to do versus letting them go because your expectations were not met. Sometimes, those expectations are necessary, and other times, they are based on fantasy. I want to encourage Seekers to take their moments of longing, after the apology is given or after the conflict has been resolved, and try moving forward. It's OK if you wished things had gone differently; you are allowed to extend grace both to yourself and the other person. Longing will only lead, however, to more longing.

Approaching Conflict with a Seeker

You may experience conflict with a Seeker because . . .

- If you are an Improver, they seem to care more about their feelings than reality
- If you are a Giver, they seem to be self-centered
- If you are a Doer, their self-sabotage feels avoidable
- If you are a fellow Seeker, you genuinely don't feel like other Seekers
- If you are an Investigator, it feels like their emotions take priority over others'
- If you are an Advocate, they seem to be inauthentic while trying to be authentic
- If you are an Explorer, they seem to create problems for themselves
- If you are a Defender, you don't know how to act around them
- If you are a Peacemaker, their emotional expression can feel blindsiding and unnecessary at times

As a Seeker, you may experience conflict . . .

- With an Improver, because you feel like who you are is a project that needs fixing
- With a Giver, because you both connect to your emotions differently
- With a Doer, because their identity diffusion seems inauthentic and insecure
- With a fellow Seeker, because it feels like a competition to see who can be the most valuable
- With an Investigator, because they seem completely detached from their emotions

- With an Advocate, because they seem to play devil's advocate for no reason
- With an Explorer, because they seem to not care about how you feel at all
- With a Defender, because desiring leadership doesn't mean you have to be cruel
- With a Peacemaker, because they seem to not care about things as deeply as you do

We can't control the behavior of others, BUT here is what you as a Seeker can do . . .

- Remember that someone's criticism of you is not always personal to who you are (1)
- Understand that others communicate love by doing (2)
- Accept that self-consciousness does not always have to lead to inaction (3)
- Have empathy for their similar emotional experience of feeling outcast, even if it looks different from you (4)
- Understand that others may have a harder time settling into gray areas (5)
- Learn that others cope with the need to belong differently than you (6)
- Accept that moving forward despite how you feel is not always unhealthy (7)
- Realize that taking breaks from intensity doesn't mean you are being inauthentic (8)
- Remember that there is no one way to care deeply about things (9)

ENNEAGRAM 5

Introduction

The most common response I hear from other Enneagram types is how little they know or understand about Investigators. Regardless of introversion or extroversion, most Enneagram 5s are loners at heart and tend to be rather private people. They pride themselves on being self-sufficient and independent, and they value these qualities in others as well. As mentioned previously, an Investigator desires a feeling of refuge above all else. Needing to be alone goes beyond a need to "recharge" for Investigators—it is a vital aspect of being able to show up in the world as their most present selves. They are professional detachers, which allows them to easily go 30,000 feet above a situation and provide rational, level-headed observations. They feel things intensely, and often disengage to cope with how intensely they feel. Some Investigators may not even realize how prevalent their emotions are in their human experience because of how removed they have become from them. Investigators are the most "in-their-head" out of all the Enneagram types, even their Head type counterparts, Defenders and Explorers. Although prone to isolation, Investigators do value community: "They can get a lot out of a little," as Enneagram expert Beatrice Chestnut says. To their core, they desire to be capable, useful, and autonomous, which means their most profound fears revolve around being useless, incompetent, and engulfed by the world.

Investigators as a Friend when Healthy

Along with the traditional Investigator qualities, Enneagram 5s become enthusiastic in nature, harnessing a boldness similar to that found in Explorers and Defenders. Far more aware of their ability to detach from their emotions, they are less afraid of being engulfed and more receptive to being accessible to those they love. As opposed to building walls, they are champions of tearing them down. Investigators in Health display a sense of authority in who they are and comfort with how they and others show up in the world. Intellectual, witty, and courageous, Investigators engage in their relationships meticulously and fearlessly, providing a lovely soft place to land for many. Equally respectful of another's need for affection, they realize their own emotions and the emotions of others will not swallow them.

Investigators as a Friend when Coasting

When an Investigator is Coasting or in a "normal" state of being, this is when their most stereotypical qualities shine through. Though they are still in their heads, they aren't afraid to open up and joke around with those they are close to. More prone to self-isolation, Investigators in this state find it difficult to feel comfortable with the needs of others intruding upon their boundaries. Others may get a glimpse of a very opinionated, even adrenaline-seeking individual in this state, but those traits are still available only to a select few individuals they choose. Investigators also may struggle with feelings of scarcity, fearing that their physical, emotional, spiritual, and financial resources might be depleted at any moment if they're not cautious with their focus. This can cause many Investigators to "disappear" from those they love, a habit displayed by the *Parks and Recreation* character Ron Swanson, for example.

Investigators as a Friend when Stressed

When I think of an Investigator in stress, I think of one of those amusement rides that look like a pirate ship–the ones you would see on a boardwalk or fairground as they intensely swing back and forth. This is because for most Enneagram 5s, there is a drastic fluctuation between coping with stress through thrill-seeking behaviors and vanishing from the face of the Earth. Many Investigators are surprised by how much they look like unhealthy Explorers when they are Stressed. Avoidant, grandiose, and seeking adrenaline, Investigators in this state are so tired of being in their head that they instinctively focus on physical sensation to the extreme degree. The kicker, though, is that Investigators can swing from their Explorer state very quickly into their scarcity mindset. An Investigator's scarcity mindset becomes the most activated under stress, also causing them to withdraw even more intensely than before. This can cause Investigators to go completely radio silent, believing that no one needs to know where they are, and no one should be allowed into their space anyway. Safety equals solitude to Investigators who are Stressed, and they will go to any lengths to achieve it.

Taking Care of an Investigator

Tip #1: *Don't give up on them*

One of the most common requests I hear from Investigators when I've asked them about friendship on my Instagram account is how much they want others to keep reaching out to them. Their statements typically don't lack self-awareness, as they recognize they are not the most responsive individuals. Investigators usually express feelings of awkwardness or intimidation when it comes to maintaining friendships, because although they are incredibly caring people, community does not come easily for them. Many of them have said they know the Givers, Doers, Explorers, and others are tired of contacting them, or that others assume that their lack of response means they do not want to be contacted. Though it is the Investigator's responsibility to communicate their feelings for themselves, a hint I can give all the types for loving Investigators well is to not give up on them. Considering that Investigators are the most "cerebral" type, many things in real life often pass them by without them noticing, including time, text messages, etc. Investigators appreciate their space, but they want their space to be shared more than they lead on.

Tip #2: *Appreciate the effort*

Because Investigators pride themselves on not needing much from others, it can be hard for them to understand when someone else needs a lot from them. Healthier Investigators can understand why others need to express themselves emotionally, but there is still the hidden fear of being smothered and simultaneously neglected by others that sabotages them from being accessible in people's lives. When an Investigator expresses themselves in a way that comes across as minuscule to you, or they let you in a little bit more to depend on them, appreciate their effort. This isn't giving anyone permission to do the bare minimum for their partner or friend, but it does mean acknowledging how difficult something might be for someone else, given their personality. It is genuinely, purely difficult for Investigators to reveal parts of who they are to those who care about them, so thank them for their effort when they work to do so with you. It is not a small feat.

Tip #3: *Support self-care practices*

Just like the rest of us, Investigators struggle with vices. Because they subconsciously work to be detached from themselves and the world in general, Investigators may have a hard time knowing their limits when it comes to some of their behaviors. Whether that be the burst of adrenaline or diving into a niche topic that they've decided is essential to their life in this moment, Investigators have extreme ways to engage their minds while disregarding their emotional or physical needs. Encourage an Investigator to take better care of themselves by planning time together that revolves around self-care and indulgence. Whether that be getting a facial or going to a restaurant that has always been on the Investigator's bucket list, making time for the pleasurable and frivolous is necessary for continually frugal and practical-minded Investigators.

Tip #4: *Lean into their resourcefulness*

A hallmark characteristic of Investigators is researching and gathering knowledge about a topic to essentially become experts, while not acting on the goals that motivated them to seek this knowledge in the first place. Though Investigators struggle to act for themselves, they are highly motivated to help, teach, and inform others. One unique way to interest an Investigator is asking them to help you learn more about something you're interested in, or to help you solve a problem. It is much easier for Investigators to bond with you when they are able to show their insight and resourcefulness. Yes, social interaction is depleting for Investigators, but it can also be invigorating for them when they feel as though they are being useful. Giving them a space to feel purposeful will build a sense of safety that allows for emotional conversations to be had.

Tip #5: *Sometimes they just need to disappear*

It was drizzling outside as Noah and I sat at the second to last traffic light on our way back to our apartment. It was our first year of marriage, both of our first times moving out and in with someone else. Though Noah and I have always fit together as seamlessly as puzzle pieces, we quickly realized that our primary ways of processing emotion were polar opposites. I am the textbook definition of a verbal processor, perhaps to my detriment. Sometimes it feels like my head is just a ton of muffled voices chattering and yelling until I talk it out, often getting to my conclusion in real time as I speak. Noah, on the other hand, verbalizes his conclusions about how he feels because he has already gone down the treacherous road of processing internally. This means that while I need to chat, he needs to be silent. Not just regarding issues with each other, but when processing any information in our lives. Over time, I began to have the epiphany that Noah was allowed to process quietly as much as I was allowed to process loudly. Sure, there was plenty of potential to compromise, but I realized how disrespectful it can be to force someone to act like you when there is no wrong or right way to approach things as nuanced as emotions.

Noah has expressed to me over the course of our marriage how much his silence usually has nothing to do with me or anything I did. His mind is where he retreats; I like to picture him cozying up on a couch with a blanket up there as he violently dissects his interpretations and feelings. To anyone who loves an Investigator, this is your friendly reminder that silence isn't always about you. There is nothing wrong with needing time and space to recover. And yes, it is important to communicate limits and boundaries within alone time, as you shouldn't be shouldering neglect, but for many Investigators, their need to disappear has less to do with neglect and more to do with survival. Growing up, Investigators may have felt like their internal world, their self-sufficiency, was the only way to remain safe in the world. Solace and retreat are vital to your Investigator's personhood.

Becoming a Better Friend as an Investigator

Tip #1: *Withholding isn't always worth it*

Investigators often feel the need to withhold emotion, information, or even aspects of themselves to remain safe and comfortable in the world. Withholding is a coping strategy for many Investigators to maintain a sense of safety and security in the world. The more they can rely on themselves, the more they are guaranteed assurance. This means that another's sharing can feel like intrusion to Investigators, even if someone is simply sharing how they feel. There is a two-way street here, which is why grace is the most important aspect of this conversation for Investigators. Investigators, compromise with your loved ones by communicating that you need time or quiet. Allow yourself that time, with limits. You must return to the world to be present for those you love. Though this feels demanding, it is a part of what makes life full and rich, and you need it as much as you need to be alone. Secondly, believe others want to hold what you're preserving. Others want in on who you are, not to be intrusive, but because they love you. Maybe they are fascinated by you. Everyone can exist and be comfortable in harmony. I promise.

Tip #2: *You are more than your information*
Investigators feel like the ideal professor in my mind: Passionate about knowledge, humble in their insights, and ready to solve any problem that may be thrown at them. As mentioned above, creating a space for an Investigator to feel useful is a wonderful way to open doors to other conversations about who they are. But I also want to challenge Investigators to see their usefulness beyond how they can inform others. Informing can be a cover for vulnerability in a lot of ways, allowing you to express what you are passionate about without having to disclose emotional or personal details. Surprise yourself by working to actively feel and share in real time. It doesn't have to be perfect. You don't have to change who you are to do so. But as your loved ones are meeting you where you are, meet them in the middle by offering up a detail or emotion revolving around yourself, too.

Tip #3: *The distraction of dispute*

It is no surprise that because Investigators are typically well-researched individuals, they don't mind an intellectual spar every now and again. Contrary to some stereotypes, Investigators do not rely on conspiracies or rabbit holes of ever-changing media. These folks are finding the TRUTH. In an argument, during a problem, there is always an answer. There is always something to uncover that would make things better than they were before. Similar to an Improver's hyperfixation on growth in relationships, Investigators can become fixated on finding the missing piece to the puzzle to move forward or to be 100 percent sure. The truth is, there isn't always an answer. There isn't always a conclusion. There may never be a cap to how much you can learn about something before giving it a try. Work to allow knowledge to cause action as opposed to a cycle of searching for more.

Tip #4: *Sometimes intention is worth the depletion*

Investigators are acutely aware of how much energy they have at any given time. Perhaps the type that struggles with setting up boundaries the least, they specialize in knowing their limits in terms of social and sensory obligation. This awareness can easily be misconstrued as being intentional with their internal and external resources. Though it is not unintentional, it comes from a place of desiring independence above all else. Investigators may struggle with measuring how committed to a friendship or relationship they will be by how much it could possibly deplete them. As an Investigator, an area for growth revolves around the idea of emotional tolerance. Being willing to be intentional in your interpersonal relationships regardless of how another person may drain you. This does not mean I am permitting you to tolerate toxic behavior from others, but I would like to see you trust your internal reservoir as opposed to obsessing over when it will be drained.

Tip #5: *Self-reliance only gets you so far*

Investigators are saving up their emotional allowance for a rainy day. Perhaps if they don't need anyone most of the time, when they really do need others, it will count far more if they've saved up for when they desperately desire assistance. The issue with this practice is that it not only creates an attitude of extremism, but also means they are out of practice in the art of asking for help. Prioritizing community in your life begins in small increments as opposed to waiting for the big crescendo to hit. The more you practice active, emotionally honest relationships with others, the less likely you will feel smothered or engulfed or neglected. Start small—once a month, ask a friend to help you with something or ask a partner for support on a task that may even be easy for you. The more you grow your emotional tolerance and the more you focus on the abundance of what is available to you as opposed to what could be exhausted, the more confident and connected you will feel to others and yourself.

Approaching Conflict with an Investigator

You may experience conflict with an Investigator because . . .

- If you are an Improver, they seem to not act on the truth they uncover
- If you are a Giver, you can't seem to get their attention
- If you are a Doer, they seem to take too long to process

- If you are a Seeker, they seem to explain and inform over processing emotions
- If you are a fellow Investigator, you feel analyzed and judged
- If you are an Advocate, they seem to want to fix your emotions instead of listening to them
- If you are an Explorer, they never seem to be there when you need them most
- If you are a Defender, they seem unreachable
- If you are a Peacemaker, they don't seem interested in your perspective

As an Investigator, you may experience conflict . . .

- With an Improver, because their convictions blind them from the truth
- With a Giver, because you feel like you need to feel guilty about your need for space
- With a Doer, because they seem to care about grandiosity instead of rationality
- With a Seeker, because it feels like there isn't room for how you feel
- With a fellow Investigator, because it feels like a competition to see who is the most competent
- With an Advocate, because they seem to need you to function well
- With an Explorer, because they seem to be frivolous with their resources and opportunities
- With a Defender, because their stubbornness feels pointless
- With a Peacemaker, because they seem to be completely satisfied with what is on the surface

We can't control the behavior of others, BUT here is what you as an Investigator can do . . .

- Remember that you can live life through both instinct and intellect (1)
- Understand there is nothing wrong with craving interdependence in relationships (2)
- Learn to take action regardless of how much you know (3)
- Remember that it's OK to express that your emotions feel unimportant, and you need time and space in order to express them (4)
- Have empathy for the mutual experience of feeling uncomfortable in the world (5)
- Remember that desiring to rely on another in a relationship is not asking for too much (6)
- Realize that viewing the world as your oyster does not always translate to irresponsibility (7)
- Understand that while you need more time, others may need to move forward (8)
- Learn to recognize that simplicity may be a blessing in disguise (9)

THE PORTRAIT OF AN ADVOCATE
ENNEAGRAM 6

Introduction

Advocates are the glue that holds our society together. Stereotypically loyal, suspicious, and cautious, Advocates find safety and security in the act of searching for safety and security. One of my favorite lines about Advocates is in Beatrice Chestnut's book *The Complete Enneagram,* when she states that 6s ". . . defensively manage their fear and anxiety through fight, flight, or friends." Advocates can be leaders and followers. Level-headed and reactive. Passionate and indifferent. Warm and petty. Advocates are a bundle of opposites wrapped up in one. They have come to terms with this internal tension by sliding the spectrum of being anti-authority to being overly compliant to authority. Authority does not have to mean the law, and can even be a group or person or belief system they believe to be truth above all else. Many Advocates are a part of close-knit communities; they're the ones to fill in the blanks for you at the drop of a hat. Advocates are known for being in a consistent state of hypervigilance, working to anticipate anything that can infiltrate the web of safety they have created for themselves. Advocates desire the literal feeling of safety–to have support and to be guided. This means that besides fearing being unsupported or lost, they fear the threats of fear itself.

Advocates as a Friend when Healthy

Pairing with the typical traits of Advocates that you see, an Advocate in Health is an unstoppable, compassionate force of nature. When they are lifted out of a state of projecting anxiety, they can trust their intuition and insight. Advocates become diplomatic, profoundly wise and thoughtful in work and relationships. They remain fiercely loyal, but no longer at the cost of their well-being. Others will notice that Advocates may even begin to resemble healthy Peacemakers as they begin to go with the flow and find peace amid the nuance. These Advocates become much more open-minded within their close relationships and are more open to changes even if uncomfortable. They are brave and bold; trusting that even if their safety net is infiltrated, they have the tools to overcome any obstacle.

Advocates as a Friend when Coasting

When Coasting, Advocates display the most prominent characteristics of an Enneagram 6. In relationships, they will maintain loyalty, self-sacrifice, and warmth, as well as leaning into a more competitive, honest side to them that is not available to others outside of their close circle. Struggling with self-deprecation and doubt, Coasting Advocates are often the most indecisive. Whether they are unable to receive advice from others or they are seeking constant advice from those they care about, an Advocate's intensity can be unmatched in this state of being. Advocates may struggle with subconsciously trying to poke holes in the opinions and beliefs of others, positioning themselves to be the devil's advocate for the common good. Though this can be a helpful attribute in many cases, to an Advocate's partner or close friend, it can come across as distrust and instability, the two things Advocates are ironically afraid of inflicting the most.

Advocates as a Friend when Stressed

Taking on many attributes of an unhealthy Doer, Advocates channel all of their anxious emotions into either becoming the best or making sure that they are in the loop of any potential changes happening in their life. Either clinging to hyper-radical or hyper-traditional beliefs, Advocates do not see a need for nuance, as there is only "good" and "bad" in their minds. Disconnected from their gut, Advocates can struggle with making very reactionary decisions, whether they are practical or relational. Getting stuck in stress is also where more phobic Advocates will come to the defense of everyone but themselves. Though they may communicate how others are at fault for how they feel, they often feel a duty to the people they despise the most. They may even feel a duty to the people that continually hurt them the most. This can lead to an

Advocate living as a vessel for others, replacing an Advocate's intuition with the preferences of those they look to for guidance. It is strange how Advocates can become misguided when they are in this state when being misguided is also what they deeply fear. The biblical sentiment of "doing what I hate" can be most seen in stressed-out, unhealthy Advocates.

Taking Care of an Advocate

Tip #1: *Embrace common ground*

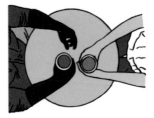

There is a coffee shop in Waco, Texas, that I used to visit in college during the rush of my Ben Rector and summer camp-loving era. It is a small, cozy building right next to the University of Baylor campus called Common Grounds. I don't know if the owner of Common Grounds is a 6, but this name is perfect for a coffee shop for our Advocate friends. One of the prized qualities of Advocates is their care for the common good while creating common ground. They are not only self-preserving in their desire for safety—often their longing for belonging comes from a place of wanting everyone to feel as though they belong in the universe. As we have witnessed throughout this chapter, Advocates tend to display many contradictory behaviors, one of them being the desire to be in the loop and question authority in opposition with their disdain for when others do so in a way they dislike. Advocates have a hard time seeing how their attitude is insulting when to them it just feels as though they are being realistic. When they see someone inquiring and approaching someone else in an unkind way, even if they agree, this genuinely affects them. Advocates above all else value kindness and embracing common ground. Advocates want every person they hold dear to feel safe and provided for. This is why when you are in the middle of a discussion with an Advocate, it is important to establish how you are approaching each other on common ground. Though some Advocates may seem confrontational, most of them avoid conflict of any kind because of how much they despise reactivity in others and themselves. Setting up a level playing field before going into any topic of discussion will be greatly appreciated by the Advocate in your life.

Tip #2: *Do not dismiss their anxiety*
Most likely, the Advocate in your life is already keenly aware of how ridiculous some of their worries are. Voicing them takes courage, especially when there is a risk of embarrassment or ridicule. You may have already noticed, based on the behavior of an Advocate you love, that they tend to make fun of themselves in the face of fears or anxieties that are cringeworthy. Though Advocates may not take themselves too seriously, they do take their concerns seriously. When they are voicing the concerns that they've already overthought into oblivion, it is a kind courtesy to not make them feel sillier than they already feel for worrying about things the way they do. There is a way to support your Advocate without enabling downward thought spirals. The most important thing you can do for an Advocate who is expressing their worry to you is to listen. I bet many Advocates can list off scenarios that have unfolded exactly how they thought they would, but no one listened to them because their concerns were too much of a "downer" or "intense." Advocates, even in the worry that feels unnecessary, may have more insight than you think; being able to be heard in full will mean a great deal to your Enneagram 6 friends.

Tip #3: *Lead with authenticity*

Within most resources about the Enneagram types, there are themes of authenticity being discussed the most with the Heart Types, specifically how much Seekers value authentic expression. While this is true, authenticity is a primary value for an Advocate, maybe even more than all the other types. Advocates lead with a simultaneously gritty and endearing authenticity that separates them from Seekers. This is because when Advocates let you into who they are, there is not an ounce of them that is pretending. When Advocates share their opinions or their feelings with you, there is no mask up. Some Advocates automatically assume that everyone also has this ability to share who they are authentically, while other Advocates really struggle with trusting the motives of another's behavior. When Advocates show up as who they are, they are expecting you to do the same for them. You may notice that Advocates keep close tabs on your actions and words, not with malicious intent, but for the purpose of seeing if you are lining up with what you've expressed to them. Leading with authenticity is a must for relationships and friendships with Advocates, because it is one of the main ways they learn how to trust others.

Tip #4: *Remind them that fear is normal*

One of the main qualities of Advocates that gets highlighted in Enneagram-related content is an Advocate's anxiety. As true as this quality in Advocates may be, it has been over-exaggerated. Many Advocates have expressed that they feel as though they are incredibly brave people, or that others don't realize how often they think of the positive outcomes before the negative ones spiral out of control. Feeling this fear has almost been sensationalized for Advocates, when the reality is that feeling fear is a core human emotion that is completely normal. A way to show support to an Advocate in your life is to not react to their fear as though it is some comical commodity to be witnessed. Remind them that fear is funny and ridiculous and normal, and you feel it too. The more that feeling fear is normalized, the more appropriate an Advocate's relationship with fear becomes. I truly believe they will begin to see how fear is not something so frightening after all because they have internal and external support to overcome moments of anxiety.

Tip #5: *Empower confidence in the face of doubt*
Whenever someone asks me what I do for a living, I rarely mention my online presence or the fact that I am a published author. In fact, being a published author is something I still can't believe I accomplished as I sit at my desk writing my second book. This is partly because I worry that they'll expect more from me than what I'm capable of–even though I am capable of a great deal, and I know that deep down, I have always struggled with minimizing my abilities for the purpose of being "realistic." Or my interpretation of realistic. Recently, I was on the phone with my dearest friend talking about something I had learned about myself concerning my career. Every single moment of confidence I feel is accompanied by this voice saying, "Well, don't feel too confident; we know how you really are." She said something that I feel is so imperative for fellow Advocates to hear:

"Christina, my hope and prayer for you is that you begin to see yourself in the way that those that love you see you."

Advocates are known for being self-deprecating. They struggle to take themselves seriously when they feel so in flux internally. The reality is, however, that the loved ones in an Advocate's life see them as a strong, capable, responsible, caring individual. Advocates truly lose sight of this in themselves. Speak up and empower confidence on your Advocate's behalf.

Becoming a Better Friend as an Advocate

Tip #1: *Keep reactivity in check*

Seekers, Advocates, and Defenders all find themselves grouped into a Stance of Reactivity. All three of these types are more likely to react first during conflict or turmoil and process how they are really feeling much later. For Seekers, this is primarily through the expression of whatever emotion they are feeling in the moment, particularly the feeling of being misunderstood. Defenders struggle with reacting with anger or frustration first and what is buried beneath the anger second. Advocates, as you might assume, struggle to react with anxiety and worst-case-scenario planning first and how they emotionally are handling the situation last. Most Advocates would say that they don't assume the worst at the beginning. In fact, the majority of Advocates have expressed that they find themselves assuming the best at first. Worst-case-scenario planning stems from wanting to be prepared for any emotion or action ahead of time, because they believe this will allow them to fully enjoy what is in the moment. Just in case what they have imagined happens, they already know how they will conduct themselves.

My challenge for Advocates who find themselves stuck in a cycle of worst-case scenario reactivity in conflict or in their friendships is to start believing that you will be able to handle whatever comes your way. When you start getting intrusive thoughts about things that could happen in your friendship or relationship, or things you are assuming are happening in your friendship or relationship, take a step back and breathe. Truly, breathe. Remind yourself that even if this worst-case scenario happens, you will be able to handle the outcome, regardless of the prep work you desire to put in.

Tip #2: *Assume less responsibility*

Advocates are known for feeling an immeasurable amount of duty to the causes and people they care about. It is practically embedded in their DNA to stand by and show up reliably even in situations that no longer serve them. "Since when are relationships about serving ourselves?" an Advocate may ask. But what many Advocates don't realize is how the feeling of obligation can sometimes disguise itself as being open in friendships, dutifully showing up without really having to show up. From what I've observed, Advocates see their sacrifice as vulnerability. That what they do, the hours they invest, and the way they are willing to be there for you against all odds is a form of opening up their heart to you. Though this can be true, Advocates can also fall into the trap of complaining about the same obligations they are passionate about. They assume so much responsibility that others do not have the space to do their part or hold their own weight. This is because taking responsibility is a coping mechanism Advocates use when their core fears arise. What if I am not safe here? What if they are not who I thought they were? What if it's all left up to me anyway? When this narrative gets continuously louder in an Advocate's head, they assume the best way to express these concerns is by assuming responsibility. This can cause Advocates to take responsibility for situations and complications that were never theirs to begin with. Assuming responsibility is a comfortable coping mechanism for Advocates, and real relational growth will come from learning to sit in the unknowns.

Tip #3: *Let go of uncertainty*

As mentioned above, sitting with the unknown is a huge growth exercise for Advocates. Unknowns, uncertainty, and uncharted territory, especially in relationships, are incredibly difficult for Advocates to cope with. As one of the pillars of friendship is intentionality, we find that uncertainty is what keeps Advocates from establishing this pillar the most. Why be intentional with someone if I don't know if I can trust them? One of my favorite quotes is from Ernest Hemingway, and I see it both frustrating and inspiring Advocates when it comes to their relationships.

"The way to make people trustworthy is to trust them."
Unfortunately, there is no shortcut to knowing if someone is a good friendship fit or a trustworthy person until you see how they handle being trusted. I believe that Advocates have an incredible gut instinct when trusting others, and my challenge to Advocates is to begin trusting that instinct. Trust when you feel like you can trust, don't trust when you feel like you can't. And if you get it wrong, that doesn't mean you are untrustworthy; it just means you're human and the other human you trusted is more complex than you thought.

Tip #4: *The distraction of comfort*

Akin to Peacemakers, Advocates desire coziness and comfort far more than they are given credit for. In fact, many Advocates are the most proactive people I know when it comes to wanting a settled space and atmosphere. Once Advocates feel settled and they've gotten in a groove that works for them, it's hard to introduce people into their flow for fear of what will happen to their routine once it's infiltrated. I want to encourage Advocates to seek community beyond what may exist for you already, even if it is just to get you out of your comfort zone.

My husband, Noah, and I have a running joke that he does this for me annoyingly well. Sometimes, Noah has a better understanding of my capabilities than I do, and he will put me in situations that push me to my limits, whether that is going parasailing or mountain biking or hiking a 14er. I groan and express my concerns and sometimes even cry. But then, once we finish the trail or hike or excursion, I look at him and say, "That was worth it. I can't believe I just did that!" Noah encourages me to go outside my comfort zone in a myriad of ways, and it has been one of the most rewarding aspects of our relationship for me over time. Because he sees all of me—the past and present and how much strength I've accumulated for future situations.

I want to encourage Advocates to step out of their bubble with friends. Or a spouse or partner. You don't have to step out of the bubble alone. In fact, some friends may already be waiting to explore or discover with you. You can do it!

Tip #5: *Give yourself support*
Whether in a compliant or rebellious way, Advocates are notoriously known for over-relying on an external support system of some kind to help guide and direct them in life. It is extremely beneficial for many to have faith or a belief system to steady them in hard times, but Advocates can struggle with taking this to the extreme, over-identifying with a system or authority figure by surrendering to it or fighting it every step of the way. This authority figure doesn't necessarily have to be a president or preacher—it can be someone very close to them in their real, everyday life. Advocates turn to others or a set of values before conversing with their own conscious mind about decisions or feelings, which can cause a breach of trust between an Advocate and their very own heart.

This overreliance on systems or authorities affects Advocates' relationships with themselves and others in their lives, especially if the "authority" in the Advocate's mind is their partner, friend, family member, etc. An exercise for Advocates is to believe that they can give themselves support in their times of need, that their gut feelings are not always untrustworthy, and that they have made more good decisions than they give themselves credit for.

Approaching Conflict with an Advocate

You may experience conflict with an Advocate because . . .

- If you are an Improver, the way they process is difficult for you to understand
- If you are a Giver, they seem to pull away from the friendship unexpectedly
- If you are a Doer, their concerns seem unlikely and unnecessary to voice
- If you are a Seeker, their desire for safety feels hypocritical
- If you are an Investigator, they seem to need continual reassurance
- If you are a fellow Advocate, you get lost in your desire for security
- If you are an Explorer, there doesn't seem to be a point to their worry
- If you are a Defender, they seem too insecure
- If you are a Peacemaker, they seem to assume the worst when it's not necessary

As an Advocate, you may experience conflict . . .

- With an Improver, because their need for rightness conflicts with your need for certainty
- With a Giver, because you are suspicious of or overwhelmed by their pursuit of you

- With a Doer, because they seem to ignore what's best for the common good
- With a Seeker, because you often sacrifice your own expression for their own
- With an Investigator, because it feels like they don't want to listen to you
- With a fellow Advocate, because you may become codependent with each other
- With an Explorer, because they perceive all questioning and concern as negative
- With a Defender, because their fear of betrayal enables your fear of abandonment
- With a Peacemaker, because they don't seem to have a plan

We can't control the behavior of others, BUT here is what you as an Advocate can do . . .

- Remember that others are not solely responsible for making you feel safe (1)
- Learn to communicate how you feel as opposed to pulling away without explanation (2)
- Understand that desiring recognition does not always mean you are vain (3)
- Take up the space you need without minimizing yourself (4)
- Remember that there must be compromise from both parties for successful communication (5)
- Have empathy for the shared experience of needing certainty; challenge each other! (6)
- Understand that growth almost always requires risk (7)
- Learn to express confidence without self-deprecation (8)
- Accept that peace can be found and felt amid uncertainty (9)

THE PORTRAIT OF AN EXPLORER

ENNEAGRAM 7

Introduction

"My whole life is working to see and feel and experience the sunshine."

My dearest friend and resident Explorer (Enneagram 7) in my life said this to me once when she was processing through some difficult things that were happening to her. Explorers from the depths of who they are desire to be taken care of so that they may enjoy and find satisfaction in life. Their deepest fears revolve around being limited, trapped, or deprived, and this is how they have gotten the reputation of being hyper-avoidant to the other Enneagram types. I've heard many of the other Enneagram types say that they wish they were Explorers, and some Explorers even agree—why wouldn't you want to be an adventurous, positive force in the world? However, Explorers are not always neon-loving bundles of energy. Some Explorers have a softer approach for how they live out their desire for freedom, taking a more emotional and joyful approach to life. Regardless of how an Explorer chases the sunshine of life, they all live with the tension of both desperately wanting to be taken care of and intensely needing to be self-preserving. This is why fostering close community may be difficult for them. Most Explorers have a large network of friends who they genuinely feel connected to. The issue that many Explorers face considering community is mistaking endless freedom and unlimited indulgence as love. The pathway Explorers opt-in on for dealing with pain of any kind is capitalizing on pleasure and the possibility of the future. The moment a relationship, whether romantic, platonic, or familial, becomes too much to bear, an Explorer feels that there is no choice but to find a route of escape. Beyond the shadow side of an Explorer, Explorers are charming, passionate, enthusiastic individuals who love celebrating others and experiencing life alongside them.

Explorers as a Friend when Healthy

Paired with their typical Explorer qualities, Enneagram 7s in Health begin to take a softer, less risky approach to life. Secure in their ability to overcome emotions, Explorers are less afraid of rooting themselves somewhere or with someone, because they are creating a life that is balanced in indulgence and integrity. Their innate curiosity becomes less about escapism and more about self-reflection and understanding; they take longer to digest their discoveries as opposed to impulsive behavior. With clearer social and physical boundaries, Explorers are not as fearful of moderation and solitude. In fact, it is within their limits that they begin to experience the rich and fulfilling joy they were seeking all along. This means that these Explorers are down for everything, but not with everyone anymore. They feel as though they have a few close friends who deeply know who they are and understand them. Though they may still struggle with feeling uncomfortable with vulnerability, they can see the positive benefits from allowing themselves to be seen, which motivates them to express their full range of emotions more authentically.

Explorers as a Friend when Coasting

When Explorers are Coasting through life, they look the most like Explorers. You can find these Explorers with friends gathered around the table, detailing their most recent story, reframing an undeniably difficult experience to their friends with a positive perspective and laughter. Though Explorers remain optimistic in this state, they also are more openly critical to those in their inner circle. They will express their sadness to you when they feel it is on their terms. A perfect example of a Coasting Explorer is Lorelai from *Gilmore Girls*. Her spirits are difficult to sink, and she struggles to take anything seriously, yet she is deeply committed to her work and her daughter. Lorelai's blind spot often comes from a place of not realizing that her need for freedom affects those around her, but she is not delusional and usually ends up coming around to a place of self-awareness. The same is true for Coasting Explorers.

Explorers as a Friend when Stressed

With their Explorer qualities at an extreme, an Explorer's endless search for pleasure and freedom can quickly become intensely hedonistic. Unable to sit still and deal with the realities of the past or present, Explorers can even disappear from the lives of those they love in favor of a new adventure they suddenly feel inspired by or called to. Simultaneously, Explorers internally develop an incessant inner critic like that of an Improver because of all the pent-up pain they are avoiding. Concerned with goodness and order, an Explorer will try to live both spontaneously and rigidly, swinging back and forth between the extremes to regain control. These Explorers may be the most fun to party or celebrate with when they are in this state, but it can quickly turn sour when demands, consequences, and raw reality return to their peripheral vision.

Taking Care of an Explorer

Tip #1: *See beyond the avoidance*
Explorers have been tokened as the most avoidant Enneagram type for as long as I've known about the personality system. There are countless jokes and memes of Explorers avoiding pain at all costs, and they are often villainized for this pursuit. Though I do not want to excuse behavior that does not serve them or those they are in relationships with, I think it is imperative for others to understand that avoidance is often an SOS signal. What those who love an Explorer need to understand is that avoidance is a sign of unbelievable discomfort. Though it may feel like a personal attack against you or your friendship with an Explorer, take it as a sign that something much deeper is going on underneath their running. What may be going on underneath the surface most likely is obvious to an Explorer. My Explorer friend once had an interaction she described to me

as, "I understand that I'm being avoidant. I see it. But I don't know what else to do. And I need help."

Tip #2: *Give them time*

Recently, my very close friend who happens to be an Explorer has been going through a tough time. I quickly noticed a shift in her mindset and behavioral patterns. Her usual effervescent self had changed to a darker mood. She started expressing how she wanted to change her career and act on some of her dreams, all while expressing how unwell she has been and how alone she feels. Every time I tried to start a conversation about what was happening, she changed the subject almost instantaneously. At first, I became frustrated with her because it looked like to me that she was actively taking part in behaviors that were not serving her. But I decided to keep showing up for her and to not bring up what she was going through until she sparked a conversation about it. Soon enough, one night on my front porch, we sat and talked for hours about everything that had been going on. Of course, my heart was breaking for how much she was carrying on her own, but I also realized in that moment how difficult it is for Explorers to speak about the things that cause their soul turmoil. She needed me to give her time because she genuinely needed time to even utter the pain out loud. So do not give up on your Explorer friends just because they are not feeling things on the timeline you would like them to. Many of them do come around—remember to be patient! Explorers care more about feeling safe than they let on. Establish emotional safety if you want them to open up to you!

Tip #3: *Listen to their stories*

It is no surprise to those who are familiar with the Explorer personality type that they are avid storytellers. Less inclined to embellishment in their storytelling than maybe Doers are, Explorers like to communicate their stories with dramatic effect. Whenever I listen to an Explorer tell a story, they make me feel like I am there experiencing it with them. Many people find the emotionality or the communication of Explorers confusing, and the biggest piece of advice I could give the other Enneagram types regarding Explorers is to truly listen to their stories. How you may envision someone pouring their heart out can be found in the grocery store run-in an Explorer is dying to tell you about, or the kooky thing their coworker did that morning explained in detail. The heart of an Explorer can be found in their stories. Though Explorers still need to own honest communication in other forms, the pathway to better understanding the internal road map of an Explorer is navigating the adventurous recap with them.

Tip #4: *Make things fun*

Explorers typically seek out a variety of stimulating activities to combat an inexplicable internal emptiness that they feel. Mundane repetitive tasks are less of a comfort to Explorers and more of a reminder that there is always more to be explored and discovered out in the world. Boring tasks, unfortunately, are necessary to survival, as we all know, so my encouragement to friends or partners of Explorers is to make the practical fun. Need to do the dishes? Create a reward system where there is a fun treat when they're completed. Want to catch up for coffee? Pick a coffee shop in a new area where the two of you can experience something new together. Showing the Explorer in your life that you genuinely see the need for adventure and novelty in their life will mean a lot to them.

Tip #5: *Give their smile a break*
I find it ironic sometimes that the smile the Explorer has that we get frustrated by is the same smile we won't give a break. What I mean is, Explorers often feel like they control the temperature of a room with their energy. They cheer us on, get us excited, they dream our big dreams with us, and then we also turn around and get mad at them when we feel like we don't know what they're really feeling. Though I do believe this is valid in some cases, it is important that we observe our own behavior in these interactions. If I want the Explorer in my life to feel like they can talk with me about anything or share the depths of who they are with me, am I allowing them space to not show up as the life of the party? Am I placing expectations on who they are and how I believe they should act?

Many Explorers receive mixed messages from their loved ones, because as much as they want to express how they're feeling with you, you also become uncomfortable when they do so. There must be a compromise, a meeting in the middle. And it's up to you, especially if you are inviting an Explorer to share their emotions, to endure the discomfort or awkwardness you may feel because it's not what you're used to from them.

Becoming a Better Friend as an Explorer

Tip #1: *Embrace limits*
In my experience, many Explorers can often mistake curiosity and gratification for vulnerability. Explorers will tell you that they are not only party animals here

for the fun and the shallow, but that they are also deep and ready to go deep with you. While this may be true, I believe Explorers like to go deep when it pertains to things that they are curious about. Whether that be an intellectual topic or the heart of someone they love, when the curiosity allows them to relish something they enjoy, it makes going deep worth it. However, when the depth requires an Explorer to be present without the gratification of their curiosity, getting them to sit still is proven a difficult task. The other Enneagram types often can feel intimidated by Explorers when they need to ask the hard-hitting questions and get real, raw answers. This is where the blind spot of flightiness can occur for an Explorer. When they begin to avoid the painstaking, uninteresting, and unenjoyable, it is an act of self-preservation alone. Many Explorers don't realize the impact that this emotional inaccessibility has on other people, especially those they are close with. Explorers run out of the jungle just before it entangles them. They find a new jungle to navigate; the beginning vines and twists and turns are much easier and more gratifying than the deep forestation. What they forget is that they've usually left someone in the original jungle who is now forced to navigate it alone. In the waiting, in the hoping, in the second-guessing and anxiety, an Explorer does not realize that the person grasping the vines in the in-between doesn't want to be entangled either. I almost envision the Explorer believing that they are no longer intertwined with the vines that choked them; what they don't see is the loved one behind them intertwined with both their own vines and the vines of the Explorer.

So, dear Explorer, I urge you to use your words. Rather than running away, say out loud,

"I am not ready to discuss this yet and I don't know why."

"The thought of dealing with this right now makes me feel trapped and anxious."

"I don't know why this is so difficult for me, but it is."

Limits do not limit you. Sometimes having limits is what frees us. You could be accessible to every opportunity, adventure, narrative and more in your life, but you may miss being accessible to those who matter most in the process.

Tip #2: *You're more than your enthusiasm*
As relayed earlier in this chapter, Explorers tend to express their heart within their stories and retellings of situations they have been through. And though we encouraged others to be more attentive to these stories for clues about an Explorer's well-being, I want to challenge Explorers in their perspective of what vulnerability is. I genuinely believe that Explorers are being vulnerable when sharing their stories. But I also believe that Explorers can learn other ways of communicating how they feel alongside their storytelling. Others may not realize that in your story lies the grander emotion you are trying to communicate about how you feel. A simple practice to try is after you share, follow it up with, "And overall, it made me feel _____." Any emotion you want, take your pick! Happy emotions can be just as vulnerable as sad ones. The point of the exercise is to begin clearly communicating your state of being, even if you don't like going into the nitty-gritty of how you feel.

Tip #3: *The distraction of endless distractions*

Though I don't believe it is as easily seen as it is for Investigators, I believe that Explorers struggle with stinginess as well, just in a different font. Where Investigators may hoard their resources, Explorers hoard themselves in a way.

They preserve their energy to pursue the amusement and gratification that they are seeking in life, which directly impacts their relationships with others, especially those who may be relying on Explorers in any way. Investigators also struggle with the idea of others relying on them, and I think this reality deeply impacts an Explorer to their core. If someone is relying on them for anything but what they feel capable of giving, what if they can no longer do everything they want? What if the world begins to have bounds and fences and walls they can't hurdle over?

Beatrice Chestnut describes this behavior in Explorers as "mistaking endless freedom as love." This is the untrue belief that ultimate love must equal no limits to anything, ever. The reality is that unconditional love does need to develop roots in your relationships. It accepts and gives grace upon grace, but it also remains firmly planted; it must be in order to be effective. If you are only conserving your energy for the fun in life, what about the richness of life? The depths of life? It may not seem fun on the surface, but it will be far more satisfying in the end, both for your soul and for your interpersonal relationships.

Tip #4: *Be taken care of*
Explorers may want to feel committed in a relationship, platonic or romantic, but they do not want to feel trapped in one. This primarily means that they want to feel as though their pace of life and independence is maintained apart from the relationship. This is a healthy boundary and pursuit to have. The issue is when Explorers conflate wanting to be self-sufficient from their friend or partner with never needing them at all. If unconditional love is rooted, there is interdependence to be found in these relationships. This does not mean that independence will be lost, but that mutual respect will be gained. It can be hard for Explorers to be intentional in relationships that feel clingy or needy. If Explorers are being honest, sometimes their perception of what is clingy or needy isn't always fair or

accurate. When a friendship or relationship is unhealthily balanced, an Explorer will be able to tell from a mile away. However, being uncomfortable does not always mean something is wrong; it may mean there is something that needs to be unpacked. Stretch yourself to depend on others and stretch yourself to be depended on. I know it is scary to let someone into your world, to be afraid of disappointment. But there is nothing wrong with needing support and being there to support someone else when needed.

Tip #5: *Grace over judgment*
From the heart of those who deeply care for the Explorers in their life, there must be grace given for those who assume that you lack depth. Because Explorers are often interested in a myriad of things to differing levels of enthusiasm, it can sometimes be hard for others to interpret how much they care about something based upon what the Explorer is expressing to them. It is easy for Explorers to forget how much their habit toward distraction or interests across many sub-jects can affect others. An Explorer might think, "It is my life and people are complex and I should be able to be who I am regardless." This is true, but it is also true that because Explorers are never really going deep with one of their piques of interest or expressions of themselves, others may assume that you are shallow. Explorers, remember that others want to experience and share in the deep parts of who you are and what interests you. I know you contain wells of endless interest, and it is important to self-reflect on how you may be coming across to others before you assume that they don't care about your depth.

Approaching Conflict with an Explorer

You may experience conflict with an Explorer because . . .

- If you are an Improver, you simply do not understand their approach to life
- If you are a Giver, they seem to not desire an emotional connection as much as you
- If you are a Doer, you become frustrated with their success despite their seeming lack of care
- If you are a Seeker, they seem to avoid meaningful interactions with you
- If you are an Investigator, they seem to be irresponsible with what they have
- If you are an Advocate, you can't have a real conversation with them without being seen as a buzzkill
- If you are a fellow Explorer, you can't rely on each other
- If you are a Defender, you seem to enable each other's bad behavior
- If you are a Peacemaker, they seem to brush everything off as unimportant

As an Explorer, you may experience conflict . . .

- With an Improver, because they seem to be determined to make you feel bad about yourself
- With a Giver, because you feel as though they don't respect your boundaries or needs
- With a Doer, because their priorities seem to be in the wrong place
- With a Seeker, because it feels like they're being petty and dramatic for no reason
- With an Investigator, because they weren't there for you in your time of need

- With an Advocate, because they seem to worry themselves over nothing and then use those worries as an excuse to not have fun
- With a fellow Explorer, because it's too much of a good thing sometimes
- With a Defender, because you feel like you always have to have a definitive stance or answer
- With a Peacemaker, because they seem to do nothing about situations they hate

We can't control the behavior of others, BUT here is what you as an Explorer can do . . .

- Understand there's nothing wrong with needing structure as much as there's nothing wrong with needing novelty (1)
- Remember that needing emotional connection, especially through hard conversations, is an important aspect of a healthy relationship (2)
- Understand that others find just as much purpose in work as you do in play (3)
- Learn that sometimes there are meanings and patterns worthy of being felt and explored (4)
- Realize others have just as hard of a time communicating their needs and feelings as you (5)
- Understand that desiring loyalty and commitment is not the same as being limited (6)
- Have empathy for each other and create a safe place to feel without judgment (7)
- Remember there is nothing wrong with needing to know where someone stands (8)
- Allow yourself to be challenged and disrupted by a slower pace of life (9)

THE PORTRAIT OF A DEFENDER
ENNEAGRAM 8

Introduction

Defenders are the least likely to mistype within the Enneagram personality system because their signs are hard to ignore. Bold, assertive, confrontational, and straightforward, Defenders are the friends we have in our lives who will go to bat for us at any time. Primarily rooting for the underdogs in life, Defenders have an innate sense of authority within them, wanting to avenge whatever injustice they bear witness to. With a core desire to be strong, to wield authority, and to be in command of their destiny, it makes sense that their core fears revole around being weak, vulnerable, betrayed, or at the mercy of someone else's control. While Defenders are charismatic, powerful leaders, their natural bent to make themselves "big" can make those they are seeking interpersonal relationships with feel small. When your personality is naturally more dominating than the other types, maintaining connections may prove itself to be difficult over time. Defenders are stereotypically known for being aggressive individuals, but at their center, you will find tenderness and warmth, no matter how much a Defender may pretend that their middle isn't ooey-gooey.

Defenders as a Friend when Healthy

Alongside their typical Defender qualities, Defenders have an air of unparalleled thoughtfulness and care for others when they are in a Healthy state of being. They harness their energy to protect themselves and extend this protection to others fiercely. Unafraid to explore more of their internal world, they also become self-reflective, pursuing a slower pace of life. As opposed to assuming they have all the information about things, Healthy Defenders are constantly learning and add an insightful curiosity to their visionary mindset. These Defenders prioritize their relationships and are less concerned with being betrayed by others.

Defenders as a Friend when Coasting

When Defenders are Coasting, you see their Defender qualities the most in their behavior. Bold and assertive, Defenders have a commanding essence when they walk into the room that cannot be ignored. They are aware of their behavioral patterns but may not understand why others are so affected by them. They struggle with wanting to feel "bigger" than others, but also feel insecure about being "too much." There is a sneaky insecurity to Defenders and their desire to be appreciated and noticed by others. They can find ways for others to be dependent on them, desiring not to simply protect others, but to overprotect them. Defenders in this state will either be your greatest ally or your greatest enemy. They will fight for you tirelessly, but it also may be difficult to feel like you have room to breathe.

Defenders as a Friend when Stressed

Defenders in Stress may begin to look like unhealthy Investigators behaviorally, which may be jarring for a Defender's loved ones. Though they still carry their instinctual Defender attributes, it may seem like they go into a mode that is reminiscent of preparing for battle. Rather than using their curiosity to reflect, they become curious toward information hubs where they can prove themselves in arguments or conflicts with others. They can become suddenly reclusive and detached; less concerned with how they feel in their physical body and more concerned about who may be coming against them. This can be a hard experience for Defenders, since they are so intuition and body-oriented; the feelings of detachment can cause them to get more aggressive because of how uncomfortable they feel. It can seem as though you are walking on eggshells when Defenders are in this state.

Taking Care of a Defender

Tip #1: *Confront with empathy*

To those who really know me in my life, it is obvious when I am frustrated. Perhaps I am easily impassioned, but I am never angry. In fact, it is hard for me to envision myself blowing up at any friend, but the inevitable did finally happen to me a few years back. In the spring of 2018, I was engaged to Noah and the stressors were constant. With shifting familial dynamics, bridesmaids' dresses, and trying to graduate from college, I found myself boiling like a kettle. Anyone who was close to me could hear the whistle quietly buzzing, and only my childhood best friend and golden Enneagram 8 had the courage to poke the bear. Enneagram 8s' ability to "poke the bear" is usually something that is weaponized against them. Certainly, it can be used to unnecessarily rile someone up, but it can also be used to get someone to speak their true feelings. As my Enneagram 8 friend confided in me while also jabbing me with bits of truth here and there, the buzzing whistle turned into a full-blown train horn. I uncontrollably began yelling at her . . . yelling to her? I was mad at her, mad at the world, mad at myself. She became a willing void for me to scream into, a solace I had not been able to find in anyone else during this time. And she took it. She took it with courage and sincerity. And she heard me. I immediately felt horrible for my angry screams, but she thanked me afterward. Because now she knew me more. She knew what I was going through more. She understood what she previously could not understand. And then she became a shoulder to cry on. She morphed from mighty protector to soft place to land in a matter of seconds, and I believe that is one of 8s' most treasured qualities in friendships. They confront us not because they enjoy it with malicious intent, but to help us get to where we need to be.

Tip #2: *Get stuff done*

This sounds like a silly tip for being friends with a Defender, but owning up to your promises within your relationship with a Defender is vital for keeping their trust. Many Enneagram 8s express frustration when others are begging them to slow down, calm down, you name it! Defenders would like nothing more than to sit back and relax, but they have created a system similar to Givers where others have become reliant on them for strength and follow-through. One of the best things you can do in your relationship with a Defender, no matter what the nature of the relationship is, is to show up and take something off their plate without being asked to. Stepping into their life and slowing their pace for them by handling something on their list that they either don't find enjoyable or that they choose to do instead of rest will communicate to them that you are just as committed to their rest as you would like them to be.

Tip #3: *Share your appreciation*

An overlooked aspect of the Defender personality type is how much they value positive feedback. Because they often get criticized for the dominating approach or big personality, sometimes the continual conversation of how "too much" they are can become discouraging. It may be hard to imagine your Defender disheartened, especially if they do not show this hurt visibly in relationships. But as much as Defenders may not understand the sensitivities of others, they have sensitivities of their own that they don't always know how to verbally communicate apart from using confrontational language. Take time to share your appreciation for how a Defender is receiving feedback regarding how they take up space. Remind them that they are not only appreciated for their strength but wanted and valued apart from their vigor.

Tip #4: *Stay curious toward their anger*
One of the signifying behaviors of an Enneagram 8 is their ability to assert their anger. Whenever I conduct polls on my Instagram account concerning Enneagram blind spots, the most common response I get about Defenders is "they're just so aggressive" or "they just seem so angry and riled up." As I type this, I genuinely feel for the Defenders in the world who have become the way they are because of what they've been through in their life. Many Defenders are nurtured into their behavioral patterns, like we all are—theirs just happens to be the loudest in the room sometimes. My challenge for anyone in any type of relationship with a Defender is to stay curious about anger. As much as Defenders harp on emotions, they are some of the most emotional, gutsy people we know. They feel things deeply. Sadness, grief, hurt, confusion, discontent. But many Defenders are not aware of how much they feel these emotions, because even they are blinded by their anger at times. Rather than always assuming that your Defender is just angry, remember that underneath their anger lies clues about what they are really feeling, even if those feelings are not clear to them yet. Your curiosity and bravery toward their anger (within reason) will encourage curiosity toward themselves in heated moments.

Tip #5: *Encourage generosity*
An overlooked aspect of a Defender's personality is their desire to take the shirt off their back to clothe the underdog. Because of their profound sense of justice, they make their presence available to those who are often in need of

shelter the most. This desire to protect usually comes from seeing themselves in the stories of the underdog, whether this comes from significant hardships they have dealt with in their life or their fear of being at the mercy of another's control. Generosity comes more naturally to Defenders than even they are aware of, which is why I would like to encourage those who love a Defender to empower them to continue being generous. Not just for the sake of the underdog, but for the sake of connecting with others in a tender way.

Becoming a Better Friend as a Defender

Tip #1: *Don't wait to feel appreciated*

If there is one thing a Defender needs but will never admit to out loud, it is to feel and be appreciated by those they love. Though this desire comes from deep within their soft center, it also is evoked from a place tainted with selfishness. Defenders, regardless of how true it is in their life, feel as though they are the ones strong-arming things for everyone. They are the ones keeping others in line, making sure things get done, and seeing to those within their immediate vicinity, making sure they are active and moving forward in life. Whether or not this pressure is welcome from others, Defenders, when in an unhealthy state, can believe that they are responsible for the development and success of those they love and the places they work. Of course, where would others be without their guidance?

The truth is that the need for appreciation can become a distraction in a Defender's relationships because they feel as though they do not need to grow if they are not appreciated anyway. If others can't see what they are already bringing to the table, it's their loss. While I'm not saying this isn't a true feeling many Defenders experience, I want to challenge Defenders to examine their need for appreciation from a distance. The need to be appreciated and the reality of needing to grow can coexist. In fact, both things can be true at the same time.

Tip #2: *Loosen your grip*

Grit. Power. Energy. Doing the damn thing.

All words that many people think of when they think of Defenders; Defenders may even use these words frequently to motivate themselves into action. Other words, like gentleness, tenderness, softness, may not be as familiar to their vocabulary. These words may even make a Defender cringe. But I want to introduce to them a new way of looking at these kinds of attributes, specifically the attribute of gentleness.

Growing up, I watched my Defender best friend learn things the hard way over and over again. One of the most impactful lessons I watched her learn was the true meaning of gentleness. When we think of this word, we may picture Snow White, singing out of her window, calling all the birds and mice to her with her tranquil, melodic tone. Truly, though, gentleness does not exist without force. In fact, to be gentle means that you are simply using the least amount of force necessary.

The next time you want to plow into a hard conversation with a partner, friend, or family member, remember that gentleness doesn't mean you are lacking in firmness. It just means you are lacking in harshness. You can be both gentle and assertive at once!

Tip #3: *You are more than how you protect*

Many Defenders believe that because they are willing to put themselves in vulnerable positions on behalf of others, that immediately translates to them being vulnerable in relationships. Unfortunately, there is no shortcut to talking about your feelings, even if you feel as though your self-sacrifice has expressed all that you needed to say. I've been in friendships with many Defenders throughout my life. I've watched them pursue physical strength and mental fortitude. I've seen them want to put their lives on the line for others, to rescue people with arms they were strengthening. But though I often felt protected by the Defenders in my life, I was always unsure if they truly cared for me. I'm obviously speaking for myself, but I can't help but wonder if some of the other types feel this way as well.

When I was growing up, the mother of a close friend of mine was a Defender. She took me under her wing and made me feel safe and empowered. I didn't think to doubt about how she felt about me, until I disagreed with her. I received a very intense, critical message from her about our diverging beliefs. My heart was breaking, and I genuinely felt scared. I felt as though she wasn't even seeing me, someone she would call one of her daughters, as she wrote this message. Blinded by the need to protect her and her family's beliefs, she no longer saw me. When I apologized for believing in something the way I did (lol what), I then slowly felt her come back down to where I was. She said that she didn't mean to come on too strong and sometimes what felt normal to her felt very intense for others.

All of this is to say, remember my dear Defenders, that there are people underneath the beliefs you are protecting. There are hearts that need your sensitivity, not just your protection.

Tip #4: *Learn to understand differences*

Whenever I've interacted with a Defender in my personal life, it becomes apparent that whether they pursue a deeper relationship with you hinges on how much you have in agreement, or how much you vocalize your similar or different beliefs. Though Defenders may not feel as though this is a fair way to judge them, if multiple people in your life had said the same thing regarding your behavior, it's time to go beyond thinking you are misunderstood. Of course, when there are oppositions in beliefs concerning a Defender's view of human rights, sometimes refusal to understand is necessary for your mental health. But if others do not feel safe to disagree with you, how is that fostering a healthy connection in your relationships? If your intentionality hinges on the sole fact of someone thinking and believing the same things as you, how is that fair to the other person?

Many Defenders may assume that others do not need to understand where they are coming from because their way of viewing the world is genuinely the most just way to view the world. I want to challenge Defenders, again, to pursue being intentional with people you would typically write off. To be intentional with the family members you disagree with. To practice gentleness. If others are being asked to accept your intensity, you can practice accepting someone's differences.

Tip #5: *Don't be insusceptible*

Grace upon grace upon grace. The idea of giving grace can sometimes be strenuous for Defenders. Why extend grace to someone who never deserved it? The issue with this way of thinking is that Defenders often assume others are going to betray or come against them as opposed to come alongside them. The act of withholding grace comes from this reactive mindset. Defenders may believe that giving grace automatically keeps them from protecting. Just because others are not going about the world in the same way that you are, because others are softer or more delicate to you than they should be, doesn't mean that grace stays on the sidelines.

Defenders, protecting your people means listening to them. Practice viewing the others you are refusing to give grace to as the underdog, instead. Adjust to softness and find that it's comfier and more enjoyable than you thought.

Approaching Conflict with a Defender

You may experience conflict with a Defender because . . .

- If you are an Improver, they seem to dismiss and dominate
- If you are a Giver, they seem to flippantly excuse their behavior
- If you are a Doer, they seem to be unnecessarily cruel and stubborn
- If you are a Seeker, you feed off each other's intensity, sometimes to your detriment
- If you are an Investigator, they care more about the sport of the argument as opposed to really getting somewhere
- If you are an Advocate, they seem to take advantage of insecurities
- If you are an Explorer, their need for control can make you feel trapped
- If you are a fellow Defender, the two of you can't see past your personalities

- If you are a Peacemaker, they seem to purposefully do things to get a reaction out of others

As a Defender, you may experience conflict . . .
- With an Improver, because they care more about being right as opposed to being just
- With a Giver, because they take things too personally
- With a Doer, because they seem fake
- With a Seeker, because you can't fix them
- With an Investigator, because they feel unavailable
- With an Advocate, because they lack confidence
- With an Explorer, because nothing and everything gets done
- With a fellow Defender, because it's a game of intimidation
- With a Peacemaker, because they seem completely avoidant

We can't control the behavior of others, BUT here is what you as a Defender can do . . .
- Learn that processing the facts before asserting your opinion is just as important as taking action (1)
- Remember that sensitivity is neutral and can be one's greatest strength (2)
- Understand that adjusting your behavior based on who is in the room doesn't always mean you are fake—it means you are aware (3)
- Learn that sometimes others need to be empowered to rescue themselves as opposed to you rescuing them (4)
- Remember that being detached from your beliefs does not mean you lack conviction; it means you are open to new information (5)

- Understand that desiring guidance and a solution that works for everyone does not equal insecurity (6)
- Remember to slow down with those who go at your pace; make sure you're both OK! (7)
- Have empathy for the shared experience of feeling as though your tenderheartedness is threatened in the world (8)
- Learn that some fights are not worth fighting (9)

THE PORTRAIT OF A PEACEMAKER

ENNEAGRAM 9

Introduction

Peacemakers tend to have the hardest time identifying themselves within the Enneagram system because they genuinely see themselves within all the types. Natural chameleons, they absorb the qualities of others and find themselves blending in to a variety of situations with ease. Their core desire revolves around a need to be connected to others and to maintain their homeostasis. This directly correlates with their ultimate fears of being disconnected and separated from the ones they love or experiencing an endless imbalance with no way out. In relationships, at work, and with themselves, feeling a sense of peace is what they will prioritize in their life above all else. Sometimes, it may look like a Peacemaker's life is far from peaceful, and that is because maintaining a sense of equilibrium often comes from working to not rock the boat in a Peacemaker's mind. Diplomatic, warm, creative, and more, Peacemakers show up in our lives secretly stubborn but also unmatched in compassion and ready to listen.

Peacemakers as a Friend when Healthy

Demonstrating the typical Enneagram 9 behaviors, Peacemakers also display an interest in self-development when they are in a state of Health. More interested in connecting to their true desires, Peacemakers are unafraid to make bold decisions that invest in themselves and their future. They begin to break out of their comfort zone and engage in their community with excitement and courage. Less prone to procrastination, Peacemakers will begin to follow through on the plans and dreams they have spoken about. Their usual passivity transforms into passion, and some Peacemakers become surprisingly daring and assertive in their approach to life. They emerge into who they are, often feeling as though they have awakened from a long slumber.

Peacemakers as a Friend when Coasting

Peacemakers display the most stereotypical Peacemaker qualities when they are in a Coasting state. Perhaps there is no other Enneagram type that coasts better than Peacemakers. Once they are in a rhythm that works for them, it is very challenging for them to get out of that rhythm, even if it is no longer serving them. Peacemakers in this state are great listeners and generally come across as accepting individuals. Behind the scenes, Peacemakers open up to those they are closest to, sharing their judgments more freely. Peacemakers are also prone to becoming busy bees when they are Coasting, meaning doing everything except the one thing they really need to be doing. This means that Coasting Peacemakers may struggle with flakiness as a friend, prioritizing their comfort and illusion of productivity over connection and confrontation. Peacemakers will also pair their quiet disposition with a resilient stubbornness that may be confusing to others in their lives.

Peacemakers as a Friend when Stressed

Peacemakers in stress pair all of their Peacemaker qualities with traits that can look like those of an unhealthy Defender. As they desire a sense of internal peace, they find that their mind cannot stop racing with potential worst-case scenarios. This can be a very surreal state for Peacemakers, because it can feel as though they are completely numb to the world and hypervigilant to it all at once. Their worry overtakes their mind, and the usual go-with-the-flow mentality they have is replaced with a desire for constant security and a sense of validation. Peacemakers may feel they are simultaneously becoming more demanding and more detached from themselves at once. Many Peacemakers have described being in a state of Stress with similar adjectives to what it feels like to be disassociated or depersonalized.

Taking Care of a Peacemaker

Tip #1: *Conflict is not easy for them*

Where Explorers fear being trapped in never-ending pain, Peacemakers fear being trapped in never-ending conflict and chaos. Everyone "just getting along" is what Peacemakers truly desire most in the world, and they will sacrifice themselves to get it. Of course, there is a shadow side to this desire, but I want to remind those who love and care for Peacemakers that the intensity to which they experience the discomfort of conflict in their bodies feels tortuous to them. There is a belief that they will never be able to exit this torture if they confront it, which is why they typically don't. It is very important to anyone with any sort of relationship to a Peacemaker to remember that they genuinely need to be reminded that you are on their team and on their side through the conflict–that your love for them is not being severed just because you got annoyed or are dealing with something hard. It sounds silly, but this profoundly impacts a Peacemaker's mental health, and they will appreciate your acknowledgment of how much they grapple with discourse.

Tip #2: *Actively listen*

Whenever I do a poll on my Instagram about how each Enneagram type feels misunderstood or frustrated, Peacemakers always confess how they feel as though they cannot express what they want to because they never have another's attention. While I address this from the Peacemaker's perspective later on, I want to talk about how I have seen this in action in my real life. Others often complain that they don't know how a Peacemaker feels—how they wish Peacemakers would speak up more. The reality is, often when a Peacemaker does finally get the courage to speak up, they end up being talked over anyway. Others do not fully listen to how they feel and instead nitpick how they communicate their wants, feelings, and more.

My callout to those who want nothing more than their Peacemaker to speak up is to be ready to receive what they give. Accept their process and how they express their concerns and opinions.

Tip #3: *Do not force decisions–give options*

One of the most amazing things I've learned in my five years of being married is the power of options versus asking for an immediate decision. Both Noah and I struggle to decide what we want to eat, for example, and I know many Peacemakers who have expressed this internal tension as well. Peacemakers continually get judged for their inability to know what they want, but I believe Peacemakers do know what they want deep down. A trick that has helped Noah and I in many cases is to list off options to each other instead of demanding a conclusive answer. Instead of asking Noah where he wants to eat, I ask him where he doesn't want to eat or what he for sure is not craving. This helps us narrow down our decisions and usually gives Noah an idea of what he actually wants.

I want to encourage others to do this with a Peacemaker in their life. Unsure of what color to paint the bedroom? What color are you sure you DO NOT want painted in the bedroom? This trick can be applied to many different scenarios, and I believe Peacemakers will slowly start to feel more connected and empowered to their true desires with time.

Tip #4: *Help them connect*

As I was hiking up the second 14er of the day with Noah, I realized I needed to speak up more. I am the sort of person, similar to Peacemakers, who loves to merge into the interests of others to show love and support. There are very few things I won't do with you to show support, and I have often gone to great lengths to do hard-core activities because Noah is so passionate about them. Hiking the first 14er was the hardest thing I had ever done physically, and when we got to the top of the mountain, I could feel nothing but adrenaline and found myself overflowing with gratitude. The hike Noah had chosen was called Grays and Torreys. This is a double-14er in Colorado, but the hike is meant for beginners. It is an "easy" way to knock out two 14ers in one day because they are right next to each other. Climbing up the second 14er, my body began to give out. I realized that even though I was proud of myself and so happy to be with Noah on this hike, this was not something I necessarily needed to do for myself to feel connected. Noah needed this. He needed the views and the physical nature of the activity to feel more like himself.

After recovering from this strenuous hike, I threw out the idea of seeing one of my favorite Broadway singers at the symphony to Noah. Though he has always supported my hobbies and interests in the past, I felt nervous expressing this one, this time. I was sharing my need. Sharing how I needed and wanted to connect. Of course, Noah did not hesitate to treat me to a wonderful evening with the stunning voice of Audra McDonald in the spotlight.

All of this to say, I want to remind those who love Peacemakers that although they may be happy going with the flow of what you want, they deserve to feel connected to themselves, and you deserve to feel connected to their interests as well. Encourage them to speak up for what they want.

Tip #5: *You might have to go first*

I have always been an advocate of the idea of "going first." Be the first person to declare how you feel, what you're upset about, why you're passionate about something, because almost always there is someone out there waiting to say, "me too." Peacemakers often express the desire to go first, but many of them shy away from the action because the risk of disconnection is quite frankly too terrifying for them. Though Peacemakers can meet you in the middle when sharing their heart, I do think there is an acceptance that with Enneagram 9s, you may have to take the first step. Say the first vulnerable thing. I can guarantee that once you get the ball rolling, you won't be able to close the floodgates you have opened.

Becoming a Better Friend as a Peacemaker

Tip #1: *Agreeing isn't always the answer*

When my husband and I were dating, he showed up as his full self from the start of our relationship. Though there was the initial phase of trying to make a good impression, he was still true to himself. He freely stated what he liked and enjoyed. He did not hide his struggles or stuff parts of himself away; he was always there, fully present with me. Whereas I, on the other hand, battled to show up as my full self. I tended to merge and agree with what he enjoyed. Not because I didn't want to share my true feelings, but because my true feelings were scary for me, no matter how minuscule the topic. Any loss of connection between us felt like a failure to me, which is how my agreeable nature to Noah seemed vulnerable and open, but was instead another form of hiding. Noah began to take notice of this, and I remember us driving together to dinner so vividly one fall evening. I finally decided to ask him his secret to being honest about who he is with me, and his answer still blows me away to this day.

"If I were to fake or agree or alter myself for you in any way, you may fall in love with a version of me that doesn't actually exist. I want you to fall in love with me, for who I am wholly. Not just the version of me that is impressive or romantic or fill-in-the-blank. And I want the same from you. I want your full self, no matter how it shows up, because I want to fall in love with the real you."

Peacemakers may wrestle with accessibility because being in agreement with others is the easiest path to seemingly connect with them. If I am an agreeable person, then it won't be difficult to have and maintain friendships. Accessibility and openness in friendship come with risk. They come with the potential of conflict and uncertainty. They come with differing opinions and approaches to life. The sooner Peacemakers embrace their full selves, even the parts they fear others may disagree with, the more connection they will find in their lives.

Tip #2: *Let your anger be seen*

In high school, I had a dear friend who genuinely made me angry. He and I would get into full-blown tiffs, which was so uncharacteristic of my usual behavior in friendships. There has been no one, to this day, who could irritate me like he could, simply because of our differing approaches to life. And when we argued, he would embrace the conflict. I would pursue reconciliation almost instantly, and he would say, "I'm not ready to not be angry with you." This felt like a foreign language in my brain. How could you not be ready for reconciliation? How could you not want the conflict to end? After almost ten years, there is one conversation we had about this that stuck with me.

I told him, "Look, I was really angry with you. I'm OK now and I've processed and worked it out. And I'm sorry for how I also acted. Will you forgive me?"

To which he replied, "I will always forgive you, Christina. But sometimes I feel like I'd actually understand how you were feeling if you'd just communicated with me while you were angry. I want your anger!"

I remember how the room felt when I heard "I want your anger." I was standing up, staring at the beige walls of the newly renovated attic in my childhood home. I stood there in silence—I don't even remember how I responded. Prior to this, I had never imagined communicating my anger to anyone, let alone a friend. And I imagine many Enneagram 9s feel the same way.

Enneagram 9s tend to downplay their anger. There is a tension inside Peacemakers between conforming to others' feelings and falling asleep to their own in the process. With so many negative associations about anger, why would a 9 want to connect to it fully? Perhaps they saw how destructive the actions of anger were in their childhood. Maybe the rumbling of it in their bones is frightening. But I am encouraging 9s to let their anger be seen, because anger does matter. Like my friend used to say, being angry means that something matters to you, whether a topic, a friendship, a conversation, etc. Anger does not have to fuel destruction; it can fuel connection.

Tip #3: *The distraction of recognition*
Most Peacemakers have a deep desire to be recognized. This doesn't necessarily mean that they desire to be center stage or in the spotlight, but this desire for recognition typically comes from a place of wanting to be considered as important in the lives of others. Their voice and dreams and needs need to be considered not last, but third, second, maybe even first.

As I've been thinking about this section for Peacemakers, I have become aware of how I emulate a similar pattern in my own life. I'll use the process of writing this book as an example. Finishing this book is MY task. My passion. Something that I'm responsible for owning. I've announced many times to Noah, my family, friends, etc. that I need to buckle down and finish the book. That I have to say "no" to things in order to carve out time to finish this book.

And yet there are moments where I look at my calendar, at all the things that have been added or events or tasks that I have committed to, and I burn with rage. Why didn't anyone stop me? Why is no one valuing this project as much as me? Didn't they hear me when I said I needed to write for this book and that was the priority?

I've come to realize, after taking a long, harsh look in the mirror, that though there is nothing wrong with wanting external support and consideration, it is my job to validate and consider myself and my projects as valuable first. I get stuck in a trap of hoping and praying that others see how much value I bring to the table without ever expressing that value confidently. I want someone to take notice of how much support I need without ever having to ask for it. I want others to consider me and my needs the way that I constantly am considering theirs. This has only led to extreme imbalance and pent-up frustration in my relationships.

This distracting need for recognition and attention is often what keeps Peacemakers from taking action on the things they need to. If they can preoccupy themselves with how no one is seeing them underneath their soft exterior, they do not have to act on the things that are begging to get done. Peacemakers, I challenge your need to be recognized with a self-reflective prompt: *How can I recognize my own strength and contributions without needing the validation of others to feel worthy?*

Tip #4: *You can survive disconnection*
One way that Peacemakers wrestle with avoidance is when they sense the possibility of disconnection. It does not matter how communicative the other party is being about their feelings; Peacemakers can sense when the vibe is off from miles away. Many Peacemakers choose to pursue reconciliation because of how much they hate conflict, but they also can avoid it like the plague when they are in a Stressed or unhealthy state of being. It is hard for them to feel motivated to be intentional with their relationships if they feel as though there is the potential for disconnection. This is a coping mechanism to not have to deal with the potential reality of being separated or severed from someone they care about. It's important to note for Peacemakers that disconnection does not always mean estrangement. Disagreement or hard conversations can often lead to more unity than before. Disconnection is not forever, and separation is not the outcome of every conflict you will have.

. . . .

Tip #5: *Get uncomfortable*

Whenever Peacemakers are referred to online, it is usually with illustrations of blankets and cookies and comfort items. Peacemakers hold the reality of being strong and cozy remarkably well, and experiencing the comfort in their life is extremely important to them. Ease will always be prioritized over difficulty, which can sometimes leave Peacemakers in loneliness and isolation if they aren't careful. It is hard for Peacemakers to accept the reality that sometimes relationships are uncomfortable and will infiltrate your routine, even if that is the last thing you want. Showing up for a friend will not always be easy and it won't always come naturally to you, but that does not mean it isn't worth it. Something may not feel comfortable in the beginning, but it might eventually be comforting to experience later. It just takes work!

Approaching Conflict with a Peacemaker

You may experience conflict with a Peacemaker because . . .

- If you are an Improver, they seem to need you as their compass
- If you are a Giver, they seem to not care about you unless you reach out first
- If you are a Doer, you don't understand why they can't just do something about their complaints
- If you are a Seeker, they seem to not be affected by things
- If you are an Investigator, they seem to be satisfied with what they have regardless of if it's good for them or not
- If you are an Advocate, they are hard to read sometimes
- If you are an Explorer, they seem to avoid acting on things that could make their lives better

- If you are a Defender, you can't get them to share their opinion with you
- If you are a fellow Peacemaker, they seem hard to talk to

As a Peacemaker, you may experience conflict . . .
- With an Improver, because they seem to try to control your decisions
- With a Giver, because they react too quickly to things
- With a Doer, because you feel like you can't keep up
- With a Seeker, because you feel like you're expected to be untrue to yourself to make them feel better
- With an Investigator, because you feel like your opinion doesn't matter
- With an Advocate, because you don't understand why you would assume things won't work out
- With an Explorer, because you feel like you're their accessory
- With a Defender, because you don't understand why anyone would desire confrontation
- With a fellow Peacemaker, because you're both shy and uncomfortable

We can't control the behavior of others, BUT here is what you as a Peacemaker can do . . .
- Remember that speaking up is important regardless of the outcome (1)
- Understand that desiring initiation from you is not unreasonable (2)
- Try viewing yourself through the lens of what value you bring to the room (3)
- Acknowledge that sometimes your behavior can be just as upsetting to someone else as their behavior is to you (4)
- Remember that as you struggle with connecting to your inherent value, others place their inherent value in things like how knowledgable or self-sufficient they are (5)

- Learn that trying to prepare for the worst doesn't mean you don't desire the best (6)
- Assert your boundaries and feelings with those who may be unaware of them (7)
- Understand that desiring confrontation can come from a place of desiring reconciliation, which is what you desire as well (8)
- Have empathy for the shared experience of feeling overlooked; let yourselves scream it out together! (9)

CONCLUSION

One of the most powerful aspects of a personality tool like the Enneagram is how much it informs us of our similarities instead of differences. Yes, every human is unique and has lived in experiences you may not understand. Yes, your friend, partner, or loved one communicates in various ways that impact you. Yes, you may process it in the opposite way of the person you love the most. But at the end of the day, I think the Enneagram teaches us that our core desires and fears, no matter how much they differ, expose us all to how much we want to be accepted and loved by those we care about the most. We want to know we are safe and so are the people we love. We want to feel connected and passionate toward our own life and the lives of others. We want to know we can grow and change with unconditional love. I hope when this book found you, it helped you see yourself and your loved ones more clearly, that it gave you a pathway forward during something challenging, or increased your empathy for a human experience that is opposite yours. I hope you have seen how the ebbs and flows of life can affect not only the behavior of your friends but yours as well.

The purpose of this book is to remind us that our mental health and our ability to take care of ourselves directly impacts our relationships, and vice versa. Though we can, in theory, survive alone, our survival has added value when it is accompanied by the souls we love. It is through these different personalities that I have found a home with so many lovely people. And I hope you feel the same gratitude as you finish this book.

"In each of my friends there is something that only some other friend can fully bring out. By myself I am not large enough to call the whole man into activity; I want other lights than my own to show all his facets. . . . Hence true Friendship is the least jealous of loves. Two friends delight to be joined by a third, and three by a fourth, if only the newcomer is qualified to become a real friend. They can then say, as the blessed souls say in Dante, "Here comes one who will augment our loves." For in this love "to divide is not to take away."

—C. S. LEWIS, *THE FOUR LOVES*

Referenced Works

Julie Beck, "The Six Forces That Fuel Friendship," *The Atlantic*, June 10, 2022, www.theatlantic.com/family/archive/2022/06/six-ways-make-maintain-friends/661232/

Chestnut, Beatrice. *The Complete Enneagram* (She Writes Press, 2013).

Beth McCord, *Enneagram Type 1: The Moral Perfectionist* (Thomas Nelson, 2019).

Acknowledgments

During the time I wrote this book, my life seemed to be constantly turned upside down. Whether with tragedy, home repairs, or poor mental health, my sincerest and deepest thanks go to Aemilia Phillips, Katie Gould, and every human who spent time in the world of *Take Care of Your Friends* at Andrews McMeel. They extended endless grace during a tumultuous season of my life, accepting my state and meeting me with patience, allowing me to complete this body of work. For that, I am eternally grateful. For their belief in this book and their belief in me!

My sweet husband, Noah. The man who continually empowers, encourages, and supports my wildest dreams. This book would not be possible without your listening ear, long hugs, and sacrifice. Thank you for always assigning deep value to the work I do before I can believe it is worthy. Thank you for regarding my passion for writing and psychology as a calling, not a silly pastime. It is always you who I want to fall into at the end of the day, and it will always be you. I love you so much!

Thank you to my wonderful parents for nurturing me from a young age to take my creativity seriously. Without their sacrifice, guidance, and support, I would be lost and frayed. Thank you as well to my precious mother-in-law, brother-in-law, and family for cheering me on and picking up the little bits I create. It means more to me than I could ever articulate.

This book would simply not be possible without the experiences I've lived through in regard to my own friendships. Whether failed or flourished, every human I have loved snuck into the research for this book. I want to thank my closest friendships, the ones that currently hold me through the waves and winds of life, for never allowing me to minimize myself or what I create. The support from friends keeps my engine running!

Lastly, I would like to thank every person who continues to follow me on social media. I know para-social relationships are becoming harder to define and navigate, but my life has truly changed because you decided to press tiny buttons on your phone screen. Thank you, thank you, thank you. For caring, for sharing, and engaging. I wish to give you all a big hug one day!

About the Author

Christina S. Wilcox is a 26-year-old author, mental health advocate, Enneagram expert, and creative. You may recognize her from her first book *Take Care of Your Type: An Enneagram Guide to Self-Care*, or from one of her Instagram graphics.

In February of 2019, Christina began creating and posting content about her latest interest: the Enneagram. Within 8 weeks, her account of 800 followers flooded with 30,000+ strangers. In less than a year, Christina had reached 90k+ followers on Instagram and found herself looking at a book contract in her email inbox.

Since then, Christina has continued to pursue her passions for writing and the analysis of behavior through the Enneagram as she works a 9-5 in Content Strategy. She hopes to continue to advance her understanding of the Enneagram while expanding her written work and online content into other mental health topics outside of personality typing systems. She currently resides in Denver, Colorado with her husband, Noah, and their puppy, Moose! When she's not writing or creating, you can find Christina indulging in cozy video games, books across every genre, and quality time with friends and family.